"If you are at the end of your marriage or the end of your rope, my friend, Brandi Wilson is a worthy guide on a journey you never thought you'd have to take."

Holly Furtick, Elevation Church

"For the one ready to overcome, this book is for you. Brandi Wilson has written a wonderfully wise, witty, and grace filled guidebook to healing, forgiving, and flourishing after life's setbacks. With refreshing vulnerability, freeing truths, and practical tools, these pages reveal the beauty of the redemptive power of Jesus."

Hosanna Wong, international speaker, spoken word artist, and author of *You Are More Than You've Been Told*

"Brandi Wilson was one of the first people to welcome my family to Nashville when we moved here thirteen years ago. Now, she's inviting you to the table, too. Come get encouraged. Come get inspired. Come discover in her authentic, beautiful story that a life that is better than okay is always available."

Jon Acuff, *New York Times* bestselling author of *Soundtracks: The Surprising Solution to Overthinking*

"An amazing thing happens while you're reading this book. At first you are walking with the author through the depths and darkness of her personal wilderness. And then somewhere along the way, you feel a shift—that the author is walking with you through your wilderness. Brandi Wilson has been there and made it through to the other side. And what she has courageously and generously done in this book is return to the wilderness—the very place where you now are—and with honesty, compassion, and wisdom, Brandi serves as your guide on the healing journey to the other side, where hope

T0049887

and perseverance arrive to help you discover and recover peace and joy."

Ramon Presson, PhD, licensed therapist and featured expert in the DivorceCare series; author of *When Will My Life Not Suck? Authentic Hope for the Disillusioned*

"It feels impossible to ever feel that you will be okay. Brandi's friendship, prayer, and words were what helped me through my darkest times. This book is everything she said that helped me get to the other side, so I know you will also be better than okay because of this book."

Jana Kramer, actress, singer, and *New York Times* bestselling author

BETTER
THAN
OKAY

BETTER
THAN
OKAY

Finding Hope and Healing

After Your Marriage Ends

BRANDI WILSON

BETHANYHOUSE

a division of Baker Publishing Group
Minneapolis, Minnesota

© 2023 by Brandi Wilson

Published by Bethany House Publishers
Minneapolis, Minnesota
www.bethanyhouse.com

Bethany House Publishers is a division of
Baker Publishing Group, Grand Rapids, Michigan

Printed in the United States of America

Library of Congress Cataloging-in-Publication Data
Names: Wilson, Brandi, author.
Title: Better than okay : finding hope and healing after your marriage ends / Brandi Wilson.
Description: Minneapolis, Minnesota : Bethany House, a division of Baker Publishing
    Group, [2023] | Includes bibliographical references.
Identifiers: LCCN 2023002688 | ISBN 9780764241413 (paperback) | ISBN
    9780764242113 (casebound) | ISBN 9781493442232 (ebook)
Subjects: LCSH: Divorce—Psychological aspects. | Divorced people—Life skills guides.
Classification: LCC HQ814 .W615 2023 | DDC 306.89—dc23/eng/20230316
LC record available at https://lccn.loc.gov/2023002688

Unless otherwise indicated, Scripture quotations are from the Holy Bible, New Living Translation, copyright © 1996, 2004, 2015 by Tyndale House Foundation. Used by permission of Tyndale House Publishers, Inc., Carol Stream, Illinois 60188. All rights reserved.

Scripture quotations labeled MSG are taken from THE MESSAGE, copyright © 1993, 2002, 2018 by Eugene H. Peterson. Used by permission of NavPress. All rights reserved. Represented by Tyndale House Publishers, Inc.

Scripture quotations labeled NIV are from THE HOLY BIBLE, NEW INTERNATIONAL VERSION®, NIV® Copyright © 1973, 1978, 1984, 2011 by Biblica, Inc.® Used by permission. All rights reserved worldwide.

The author is represented by The Fedd Agency, Inc.

Baker Publishing Group publications use paper produced from sustainable forestry practices and post-consumer waste whenever possible.

23   24   25   26   27   28   29   7   6   5   4   3   2   1

For Jett, Gage, and Brewer—
you three have my heart.
We will forever be Us Four.

Contents

Introduction

Here We Are

I think it's fair to assume this is a book you never expected to need. To put it bluntly, it's the book I never wanted to write. The first thing I want you to hear is *I'm sorry*. I'm sorry for your heartache. I'm sorry for your shattered dreams. I'm sorry you're putting the pieces of your life back together.

Next, I want you to know you're not alone. Walking through a divorce is annihilating, even when you're surrounded by a loving support system. Your heart is broken, your marriage has ended, your next steps are unknown, yet the lives of the people around you continue as yours is falling apart.

If we could, I'd sit across from you at a quaint little coffee shop in my hometown and listen to you share your disappointment, hurt, fear, and anger. The opportunity to sit across from you and say "me too" would be a gift. To hold space for you to share how you arrived at this undesirable title of "divorced." Since we probably won't get that opportunity (though if you're ever in Nashville, let me know), I'm going to do my best to pour my "me too" into the words on the following pages. To create a book that doesn't give a cookie-cutter formula for moving forward, but the story you get to create by taking your best next step. While I might not know you, my heart aches for you and what you're walking through.

Feel all those emotions, friend. Tell me how you never walked down the aisle expecting to divide your household items a few years later. Admit how you never had children to parent them part-time based on a court-ordered parenting plan. Share your disappointment, frustration, and anger.

While I empathize deeply with what you're facing, I also want to pour a healthy dose of encouragement into your hurting heart. You will survive your divorce and come out stronger. Trust me. I want you to say that to yourself.

I will survive my divorce and come out stronger.

Again, this time like you mean it.

I will survive my divorce and come out stronger.

Better. One more time.

I will survive my divorce and come out stronger.

YEAH, YOU WILL.

You will, I know it in my bones. There will be days you don't want to get out of bed. Days you feel like nothing is going right in your life. Days the grief hangs heavy over your slumped shoulders. And also.

There will be days when you begin to see glimpses of yourself again. Days you recognize how far you've come. Days you celebrate the hope you begin to feel. Days when tears don't roll down your cheeks, and (believe it or not) you catch yourself laughing again.

I'm sorry these are the circumstances that introduced us, but it's an honor to be on this journey with you and to write a book that whispers hope into your heart once again.

The year 2016 was the year my husband walked away from our marriage. It was a doozy of a year, to say the least. A year I never expected to experience. Let me give you a quick glimpse into my life pre-divorce.

I married my college sweetheart. Very early into our marriage we planted two churches, the latter being Cross Point Church in Nashville, Tennessee. The church boomed in growth and so did my pastor-husband's career. In fact, the church spent numerous years listed as one of the fastest-growing churches in the nation. Nashville is a city of dreamers, young and old, and the church matched the environment and atmosphere of Nashville perfectly. As the church grew, it expanded to five campuses across Middle Tennessee.

In 2016, my then-husband announced that he was resigning from the church. His departure from the church and our family played out on the front pages of local, state, and national publications. The first paragraph of the news story in *The Tennessean* put it like this: "[The pastor], who founded Cross Point Church 14 years ago, said he resigned as senior pastor of the Nashville-area megachurch because he is tired, broken and in need of rest."[1]

Meanwhile, behind the scenes, I was dealing with some painfully private things that the readers of *The Tennessean* weren't privy to.

The narrative being repeated was about an overworked pastor who was burned out. The reality was I'd been sleeping alone, not by my own choice, for more than six months. In my heart I was sure my suspicions were correct; the brokenness went much deeper, trust had once again been broken, and I was experiencing devastating heartbreak.

And the reality is I didn't just lose my marriage and family unit; I lost my church family. The people I'd spent the last fourteen years leading and loving. The staff I shared a meal with every week at staff meetings and regularly invited into my home. The ladies whom I'd had babies alongside and raised our children together. The church that wasn't just a job or role to me, but a spiritual extended family that I loved and was honored to serve.

One Sunday I was at one of our campuses hugging people, and the next Sunday I was hiding out in my home telling my kids their dad didn't work at the church anymore. It wasn't just my marriage that unraveled. Life as I knew it had ended. I'm aware that my divorce was more public than most divorces are, but I've talked to enough women to know divorce always plays out in some public way for everyone, even if it's just in the neighborhood, the family, on Facebook, or under the steeple of your church. The unraveling of your family unit is traumatic, and it can often feel like all eyes are on you.

Because my divorce played out in public more than I was comfortable with, deciding to write this book took some time. Write it too soon and I'd be writing out of wounds, which isn't healthy for anyone. I decided to take some time to heal. Writing from my scars allows a level of empathy anyone walking through a similar situation deserves.

This book isn't about why my marriage ended. It's about what God chose to do in me as I chose to begin again. It's about mending broken hearts and stepping boldly into a new identity. This book isn't about what happened to my marriage—but about who I have grown into. This book isn't about what was lost—but what I've found. This book isn't about what was taken from me—but what remains. Better than okay is a life where you're not the victim but the victor.

As we walk this path toward hope and healing together, I'm going to occasionally include portions from my personal journal. Not only was writing a huge part of my healing, but the journal entries also give you a glimpse of what I was feeling and hopefully will allow you to feel a little validated in your own journey and emotions. You're not alone, and you're gonna be better than okay.

Dear 2016,

I AM NOT SAD to see you go; you were the roughest year of my life . . . full of heartache, disappointment, betrayal, and loss. There were days when I didn't want to wake up—didn't want to face life. But by the grace of GOD—I DID. I got up and moved forward every single day. My marriage was over, my friendships drastically changed, and I realized TRUE TRUST was something I would have to relearn.

My heart literally ached from the loss I experienced. But you, 2016, also brought lots of GOOD. I thank God for reminding me to FOCUS ON THE GOOD. He is my ultimate good and He surrounds me with glimpses of His goodness every single day.

2016—YOU SUCKED. But you also began to remind me WHO I AM, who God uniquely created me to be. You reminded me who I am in Him, not defined by my marriage or my connection to a thriving church, but by my identity in Christ. I remembered I am witty. I love to be silly. I love to feel physically strong. You taught me to love yoga and made it medicine for my heart and mind. You started teaching me about true FREEDOM. I pray that I always show my boys how to live life FREE.

2016—You threw a lot at my kids. As much as my heart ached for me, it was broken for them. I hate any of the hurt I have caused them. My prayer is for them to grow through this and for us to draw closer together, this new little family.

Good-bye to you, 2016.

Good-bye to the pain, the heartache, the hurt, and the betrayal. Good-bye and good riddance. I never want to look behind me, but I always want to remember all you taught me.

—B

1

To Be Continued . . .

How to Walk into the
Unexpected Episodes of Life

Sitting in an office decorated with stiff, dark leather chairs and walls painted a depressing shade of beige, I took a deep, shuddered breath. The pen in my right hand lightly grazed the paper and signed my full legal name: Brandi L. Wilson—the name I'd signed thousands of times since the moment I walked down the aisle of my parents' church in tiny-town Kentucky toward the man I loved. A walk toward the person I planned on spending the rest of my life with—to have and to hold, from this day forward, for better, for worse, for richer, for poorer, in sickness and in health, to love and to cherish, till death do us part. A walk that signified a beginning full of hopes and dreams for our future.

This time, the signing of my name signaled an end. An end to my marriage. An end to my current family unit. An end to being a wife. An end to my role at a church I loved and helped plant fourteen years before. My signature would end life as I'd known it. Signing my name signified my status as a divorced woman and a newly single mom to three sons.

Yet here I was. Sitting in an attorney's office after ten hours of mediation. Feeling a mind-reeling mix of emotions. Intense relief and immense sadness. Pride that I had made it this far and terrified of all I needed to figure out. Hopeful that the best was still to come and mourning all that was broken and lost. Signing my name for the first time since I was twenty-two as a single woman.

No one foresees their marriage ending in divorce. No one expects to live through the division of a life you worked hard to create with the person you loved. Splitting Christmas decorations, kitchen appliances, furniture, savings accounts, and—the most difficult—time with your children. No one delivers a baby, looks into that infant's eyes at the hospital, and thinks, *I can't wait to spend every other weekend and even-numbered-year Christmases with you!*

I never expected this to happen to me. Me, who became a Christian at a young age. Me, who had been in church since birth. Me, who had chosen to follow God's call in my life. Me, who served a church with my whole heart. Me, who believed in love. Me, who was created to value the connectedness of relationships. Me, who was loyal to the core. Me, who loved and adored her husband and had since I was nineteen years old. What the heck was happening?! Signing those papers and recognizing I was now divorced felt like an out-of-body experience.

Putting into words all the emotions bubbling inside you when facing divorce is incredibly difficult. I come from a long line of couples who are happily married. Parents, grandparents, aunts, and uncles all successfully married and enjoying decades together. Divorce wasn't an option for me. Hard work, counseling, figuring it out, sticking through tough times, communication, and dare I say *love* were what I believed in. However, it takes two people committed to doing the work, individually and together. Unfortunately, from my perspective, I was the only one who wanted our marriage to work out. I felt (and still feel) I was the only one who was committed, who desired to do the hard work of healing, who was willing to forgive, who wanted to keep walking through life side by side, hand in hand, together.

Signing my divorce decree was like reaching a finish line marking the end of an eighteen-month battle. I was now facing a new beginning where everything was unknown. I'd already been through so much devastation, and I was too tired to even think about starting over. Physical, mental, and emotional exhaustion regularly overpowered me and brought me to my knees.

Maybe you're like me. I'm a glass-half-full, let's-find-the-positive-in-this-situation kind of girl. I'm not one who likes to focus on suffering. Yet we all go through seasons of suffering that feel like they are going to take us out, cause us to wonder if we'll survive the heartache, force us to question what we believe and who really loves us. Trust me, I wish I didn't have to write about divorce and suffering, but I choose to share the value a season of suffering brings to your life.

Back in the days before we could binge-watch entire series on Netflix or Hulu, television shows and movies would occasionally reach a cliffhanger—a place where you don't know how the story will end—and then the three looming words *To be continued . . .* would flash on the screen. Then we waited. Sometimes the waiting would be seven days for the next episode to air, and sometimes we waited four months (*gasp*) until the next season started the following fall.

The medical drama *Grey's Anatomy* did this so well in season 2 episode 16, which aired after the Super Bowl in 2006. I'd watched the game with a group of friends, and all the men had exited to the kitchen to finish off the remainder of the snacks while all the women eagerly gathered around the television, because Mc-Dreamy, duh. I remember exactly how I felt watching the beloved protagonist, Dr. Meredith Grey, go from assisting a paramedic in the operating room whose hands were on a bomb inside a patient's chest cavity (yep, it was a very realistic medical scene) to putting her own hands on the bomb in the patient's chest! Cut to a black screen. And you guessed it: *To be continued . . .*

Those three words left audiences full of anticipation and questions. Then we waited. *To be continued . . .* left us wondering what was next. What was next for Dr. Meredith Grey? How would Meredith move forward in what appeared to be a hopeless situation? Would she survive? Was the bomb going to explode in her hands?

My life felt *To be continued. . . .* My story would continue, but what my future looked like was up in the air. What was next for me? How would I move forward when I felt so empty? Would I ever feel happiness again? I wanted to curl up in a ball and sleep until it was all over. The dismantling of my family was an overwhelming and traumatic process to live through. Everything around me existed as painful reminders of my heartache and loss. *Suffering* was the only word to describe the trajectory of the path my life was taking.

To be continued . . . creates suspense and frustration. We just want to know what happens and if everything will be okay! But one other perspective on *To be continued . . .* is that it brings hope. It is not over. There is more for you. I understand that might be hard for you to believe, but I'm six years down the road and want you to know there is a future where you will smile again. What you thought was the end wasn't; the story continues. And that hope may feel small—the future might seem daunting and overwhelming to you right now, but there is always a seed of hope in every *To be continued . . .* no matter how small.

One person who models hope in the midst of suffering is Anna the prophetess, mentioned in the New Testament. In three simple verses, she presents a model for walking through suffering.

Anna enters the story when infant Jesus, only forty days old, is being presented by His parents at the temple. Luke writes, "Anna the prophetess was also there, a daughter of Phanuel from the tribe of Asher. She was by now a very old woman. She had been married seven years and a widow for eighty-four. She never left the Temple area, worshiping night and day with her fastings and prayers" (Luke 2:36–37 MSG). Anna then approached Mary, Joseph, and Jesus and began thanking and praising God. She "talked about the child to all who were waiting expectantly for the freeing of Jerusalem" (Luke 2:38 MSG).

We don't know a lot about Anna. Her story is recorded with only three brief verses, but we can gain great insight into how her suffering strengthened her and brought her closer to God.

1. Anna chose worship over bitterness

Anna lived in an era when being married meant security, identity, and provision. Her husband had passed away decades before, when she was a young woman. Scripture says she was a widow for eighty-four years, living at the temple. *Dear Lord, please help me to not be single for eighty-four years!* Sorry, I just like to shout that prayer up on a regular basis.

Anna was on her own. Yet somewhere during that difficult and heartbreaking journey, she made a decision. She wasn't going to live a life of bitterness and disappointment. Instead, she was going to live a life of worship. At a time in her life when she had every right to complain, to have a short temper, to speak hurtful words, to doubt, to choose bitterness, she decided instead to spend her time worshiping. I'm sure she had her moments. Anna probably grew tired at times, wondering how much longer she'd be on those temple steps. Regardless of what she felt on the inside, she chose praise.

2. Anna was committed to hope

She knew her story wasn't over; it was only to be continued. She held on to hope that a man would come to save her and the whole world, and she waited her whole life in anticipation of that promise. One thing that strikes me is Anna obviously didn't have a kinsman redeemer—a male family member who, as the nearest relative, was charged with the duty of taking care of her. There wasn't family who stepped up to help her out.

Luke 2 says she never left the temple. She was committed to seeing the story of salvation and redemption play out in her life.

3. Anna saw God in places where others didn't

The suffering changed her and changed her perspective. Anna's personal tragedy had driven her to God rather than away from Him. She had drawn close to Him in the difficult years and trusted that He was with her right in the middle of her personal tragedy.

So when the Savior of the world came to the place where she worshiped, she recognized him immediately, even though He was only a few days old. She had been focused on God with all her mind, heart, spirit, body, and time. Because she lived a life of worship, anticipation, and hope, when the promise over her life was fulfilled, her eyes were wide open to it.

We follow a suffering God who is with us in every experience of our lives, especially when we're suffering. Our challenge is to allow our dark times to draw us closer to Him so that we will see Him at work in a way others might not. When you're leaning on God, He begins to open your eyes to see beauty in your brokenness. Trusting Jesus in our pain sharpens our spiritual vision to recognize Him at work and share His faithfulness with everyone who crosses our path.

When I was so desperate that all I had was God, I poured out my hurt to Him regularly in the pages of my journal. In a lot of ways, God was the only person I felt I could be totally honest with. The pain felt like my heart was breaking, and having trivial conversation was exhausting, so I often hunkered down in my house, alone. Depression ruled my days, and anxiety stole sleep from my nights. It was a period of my life that I hoped would end quickly . . . but I also knew the battle that lay ahead. My intention became focusing on one day at a time. Anything else overwhelmed me and seemed insurmountable. Fear and anxiety were my constant companions; the questions swirled day and night:

Would my heart ever heal from the repeated betrayal and abandonment?

Were my children going to be forever damaged from the impending divorce?

Would I be alone forever?

Would I be able to make it financially?

How would I pay for college as a single mom?

Had I made the right decision to file for divorce?

I asked myself that last question repeatedly: *Did I make the right decision?* The right decision for myself and the right decision for my boys. Divorce wasn't what I wanted; I desired to continue to fight toward reconciliation and restoration. But what I wanted wasn't to be. I realized I couldn't control what was happening to me, but I could control how I responded to what was happening to me. That began to help me feel a bit empowered. Life felt out of control, but I did have control of myself and the life I chose to live moving forward. I began to see glimpses of hope.

Because in my suffering I knew He was my lifeline.

In my suffering He was my constant companion.

In my suffering He was my HOPE.

I'm not going to pretend like leaning in to Jesus was easy. Doubt resided in my head, and I spent many hours begging God for the resolution my heart longed for. Why wouldn't He give me what I asked? Could God *really* be trusted? Did He *really* desire for me to live life to the fullest? Because it sure didn't feel like it. Could anyone *really* be trusted? Did He *really* want what was best for me? There was so much I didn't understand, and I questioned where God was and why He had allowed my life to fall apart. Why had God permitted my kids to endure the pain of their parents' divorce and the loss of the only church family they had ever known?

Rejoicing in heartbreak sounds like an oxymoron, but it's heartbreak that will prompt your soul-searching and be a catalyst for your closeness to God. God will help you stand in your pain, not because of your strength but because He is in you. You who have begged for the pain and heartache to end, who are so overwhelmed—look to Him, keep your head up, cling to hope, ask Him to help you learn from this suffering and to see what He wants you to see. Don't just look, but see Him and those around you.

If you were waiting to find out what happened to Meredith Grey, I'm here to tell you she's still alive and well in season 18 (the continuing never ends). In *my* current season, the suffering is a lot less intense. There are some seasons of suffering that force you to figure some things out but that don't completely deplete you.

I don't know what season you're in. Whether the suffering in your life feels too overwhelming to function, you feel depleted, or you are in the process of recovering from a season of intense suffering, know that this is not the end. The words *To be continued . . .* are for you and for your life, and there is immense hope in those words.

Suffering knocks us down, but it brings us to our knees in prayer. Suffering will take your breath away, but you're going to cling to Him like never before. Suffering will leave you emotionally depleted, but you're going to whisper the name of Jesus. Suffering will make you go to places you never wanted to go. But you can do it! Suffering gives us the opportunity to become investigators of our own lives and find beauty in our brokenness. To see God at work in ways we never would have dreamed. Sharing our suffering allows us to take our failures and faded desires and bring others on the journey to finding hope in Him.

In order to truly heal, I strove to embody this quote from Henri Nouwen: "You can tell your story from the place where it no longer dominates you. You can speak about it with a certain distance and see it as the way to your present freedom. . . . Your past does not loom over you. It has lost its weight and can be remembered as God's way of making you more compassionate and understanding toward others."[1]

As I signed "Brandi L. Wilson" as a newly single mom, I knew I was damaged—but not destroyed. Moving forward wouldn't be easy, and life would never be the same. But deep down, I knew I could and would begin the process of healing and would rise again.

I've made a surprising discovery since that day: There's good news when your life falls apart. Really. The beauty of your life falling to pieces is that you get to put those pieces of your life back together the way you want with the help of God. Yep, you're in total control. You have control of your thought patterns, your self-care, how you spend your time, what you want for your future, and how you act on your feelings. It may not feel like control at the time, since it's thickly laced with fear and apprehension, but it is control. And when we take that control and choose healing, hope, and closeness to God, we will begin seeing a lot more of God and His promises in our stories.

You might be going through hell right now, but you're going to be okay. You really are. Just take one day at a time. Let me remind you of a few things you might need to hear.

You are worthy.

You are loved.

You are strong.

You are going to make it through this.

You are unique and special.

You will survive your season of suffering and come out stronger.

You're going to be better than okay.

2

Pretty Scars

How to Find Beauty in the Wounds

My girl Taylor (Swift, for those of you who aren't fans) begins her song "Love Story" describing what it was like to be young when she first saw her love . . . and that's about all that aligns with my personal love story.

My personal love story. This is possibly the hardest chapter I'm going to write. I've been putting off this chapter for months and actually skipped over chapter 2 to move on to chapter 3. But by the time I got to chapter 11, I knew I needed to do this—for you, but also for me. Today, as I decide to tackle it, I've already paused and taken a few deep breaths. The brief reflection is already causing anxiety to course through my body; my chest is tight, and my heart is beating a little faster.

A flash-forward to the end might be a good place to begin. By the pool at a well-known resort in Las Vegas, my ex and I were surrounded by hundreds of strangers when I heard him tell me he had never really loved me. I had a book in my lap and tears running down my cheeks. To be told after spending three years of dating and nearly twenty years of marriage with someone that they never really loved you, that's a hurt that is hard to reconcile. The tears came because the words I heard were not how I remembered our story. Honestly, our initial meeting and the months that followed are pretty vivid in my mind, and what I do know is my feelings were genuine.

I want to pause here and pull out of the story for a second and say something very direct. Your ex may say things to you that aren't true to relieve their own guilt over the hurt they are causing you. They may rewrite the narrative to justify their actions or decisions. If something they say feels like it comes out of left field, take time to evaluate if they are saying what is true or what takes away their discomfort, their guilt, or their shame in the moment. Now, back to the story.

Here it goes. My sophomore year of college I became friends with a girl who lived down the hall of my dorm at Western Kentucky University—yes, home of the infamous mascot known as the Hilltopper who, in actuality, resembles the vintage McDonald's Fry Guy character. My journey at WKU began because my high school boyfriend was on the football team and I decided Western would be a good next step for me. Yes, I followed my high school boyfriend to college. It was a small-town-football-captain-and-head-cheerleader romance. He was a great boyfriend; I have a lot of fond memories of that relationship. But once I left the small town, I realized there was more out there for me: more people to meet, more places to explore, more dreams to chase, more life to be lived.

Back to the girl down the hall. Her name was Andrea, and we met going through sorority rush together. My boyfriend and I were on shaky ground, and things were slowly unraveling, when Andrea invited me to go home with her for the weekend to McLean

County, Kentucky, for her high school homecoming and to get some incredible home-cooked food. With my relationship falling apart, it seemed to be a great time to get away and clear my mind for a bit. One Friday afternoon in October, I loaded into Andrea's car with a bunch of strangers and hit the road to her parents' house.

It was on that two-hour drive through the back roads of Kentucky that he and I first met. It was unexpected, special, and unique. When I met him, his head was actually shaved. (He was working as a youth pastor, his student ministry had reached an attendance goal, and as a result, he shaved his head.) He was the opposite of the boys I had grown up dating. He was charismatic, engaging, and appeared serious about his personal faith. I found that really attractive—a nineteen-year-old guy who wanted to reach others for Christ. Another young person who thought about others and wanted to create positive change. He was also entertaining. I realized I was a sucker for someone who could make me laugh and engage in conversation that was more than surface level.

That's how it started: some innocent flirting and conversations about what we both wanted for our future. A connection was created. Driving back to college that Sunday, I knew life was going to be different and an adventure was beginning.

The unraveling relationship with my high school boyfriend took a nosedive upon my return from that weekend in small-town Kentucky. The world already appeared bigger than what I had previously experienced, and I wanted to run full steam ahead through doors that were opening.

Once I was officially single, his pursuit began. I even viewed that as a good sign—that he'd waited until I was single to make his move.

Those early days were wonderful. We carved pumpkins and took walks through the snow together. We sent loving cards to each other and planned romantic dates that we knew the other would love. We watched a lot of movies at the dollar theater and shared many meals of Kraft Macaroni & Cheese with a side of original flavored Doritos. We were twenty and in love. Those early days led me to believe that we would have a long, full life together and do big things side by side.

We quickly began to do big things. It was the mid-1990s, and Rick Warren's *Purpose Driven Church* was changing the scope of what traditional church had represented in America for decades. I knew when we began dating that he'd been called to ministry in the local church. After we both quickly devoured Rick's book, we had more direction and a blueprint for what was next.

We were going to start a church. At twenty-one years old and joined by four other families, we planted a church in small-town Kentucky. He was a lead pastor for six months before we were married. And minus the legal documents, I functioned as pastor's wife before walking down the aisle. At our wedding we already had a church of a couple hundred and were part of seeing God move and transform people's lives. It was exhilarating, challenging, and fulfilling. I landed a teaching job at the local elementary school, we got a puppy, we both were working on our master's degrees, and we were building a house.

We were living the dream. There's something about falling in love when you're young that makes you believe you can conquer anything together. That things will be different for you. Hardships won't hit you. Divorce won't divide you. Rough seasons will bring you closer rather than tear you down. Together you're invincible.

There's also something about falling in love young that means you're growing up together. Two kids figuring out life one day at a time. Embracing responsibility and making choices together.

Sharing adult-size dreams for your future as you're cheering on and supporting the other as they move toward their dreams.

We fall into love, optimistic and hopeful. My guess is that your love story might have some similarities to mine. The details are different, but you remember the emotions, excitement, and elation of early love. You experienced the butterflies when he looked at you, and a smile crossed your face when you locked eyes across the room.

Our stories are different, yet so much can be shared. I've often thought the strength and connection of community isn't what you *have* to say but what *doesn't* have to be said because the other person "knows" what your life looks like behind the scenes.

Yes, our stories may be different, but I know what your life looked like behind the scenes. The love story you never foresaw losing. The divide you never desired. The heartbreak you never anticipated. And yet here you are, your marriage is ending or has ended.

Where does that leave us?

What's next?

Will I be okay?

Regardless of what he said that day lying by the pool at the resort, we had been in love. He had loved me as much as he was capable of loving anyone else. And I had loved him. At that moment in time, though he had crushed my heart, I still loved him. We had shared beautiful moments of love and life together, created three incredible children, and had made significant and substantial memories side by side. After twenty-three years together, I knew him better than I knew myself. There were times I wasn't sure where he ended and I began, our lives were so intertwined.

And he was choosing to walk away from it all—all of our past and the future we could have created.

While some parts of that day by the resort pool are vivid, others are hard to recall. I can't remember how the conversation ended, who got up first, or even how "normal" conversation resumed. I do remember getting showered, dressed, and going to dinner with my best friend, Lori Wilhite, and her husband, Jud, that evening. My heart was crushed, I was struggling to function, and my husband acted like nothing was out of the ordinary. Hours before, I'd heard the words that he had never loved me, yet now we sat at dinner like the conversation had never happened.

It felt like an out-of-body experience. I had an open, gaping wound. My heart had been torn wide open—not the way a surgeon precisely slices using a scalpel, but gashed open with words and actions that felt vengeful and appalling to me. Sitting across the table from my best friend, I smiled, tried my best to engage, and ultimately pretended my way through dinner.

Pretending was becoming a pretty natural state of existence for me. But inwardly I was scarred. Unsightly scars were covering the last twenty-three years of my life. All my best moments and memories were scarred. The gashes made by the words from earlier that day weren't going to heal quickly, and nothing about my life in that moment felt worthy of a second glance. Sitting at the table that evening, there was so much I didn't know.

Most important, I didn't know that when something is removed from our life, it *can* be for our good.

———

Like most teenage girls, I spent a lot of my younger years trying to tan. I use the phrase "trying to tan" because I have strawberry blond hair, fair skin, and loads of freckles. The freckles have faded a bit since I've "matured," but they brighten in the summer and make me feel like a kid again.

Why am I filling you in on my physical attributes? All my tanning in the 1990s, plus my fair skin, plus ignoring my mom's repeated plea for sunscreen application = lots of skin cancers.

My first skin cancer was removed six months after the birth of my first son. Since then, I've been getting full body checks every six to twelve months. Here I am, twenty-one years later, sporting seventeen scars from removals. It goes without saying: Listen to your mother and wear your sunscreen. And don't forget to reapply every sixty to ninety minutes, people.

Recently I had two skin cancers on the bicep of my right arm. The same doctor has done all my excisions, so I'm comfortable with her surgical routines. However, this time when she stitched me up, she used a different method. The sutures were in the shape of a cross. They sit a couple of inches apart, a little catty-corner from each other. Once the swelling started to recede, I realized the incisions were healing a smidge lumpy. Not because anything was wrong, but because the healing process this time around was different. That smidge of lumpiness became even lumpier when the swelling fully dissipated, and I wasn't happy with how these scars were shaping up. Luckily, before I had too much time to get full-blown obsessed with their irregularity, it was time to get my sutures removed, and by then I was super curious to see what my doctor had to say.

Upon asking my doctor about how the cross-shaped scars were healing, she responded, "They're healing great. They look rough right now, but I use this method because it creates a pretty scar." That phrase got my attention.

A pretty scar.

Such an oxymoron. Scars signify something had to be removed. Something was taken away. Scars remind us where we've been wounded. Scars convey we had to be put back together. Scars represent hurt, bleeding, and repair. The scar is a lingering indication of where impact occurred. None of that sounds very pretty.

And scars are also a product of healing.

A scar is the body's natural way of repairing what was lost or damaged. Creating a new layer protecting the prior wound. Scar tissue is made of fibers, not skin cells, making it stronger than original skin.

Reflecting on my life—and specifically the loss of my marriage more than six years later—I see a pretty scar. The reality is that the amount of loss was immeasurable. The impact of heartache, loss of relationships, secrets, and torment was immense. The gashes left ugly marks, and the healing wasn't always smooth. Triggers from the trauma overflowed into all areas of life, and crying felt as normal as waking up each morning.

But trust me when I tell you the growth in the midst of healing is beautiful. The development of emotional strength—finding freedom and the value of my individuality—outweighs the pain. Here's where you reach a crossroads. Internal scars are easier to hide and easier to deny. You get to make the choice to face your grief, process your anger, and begin to heal.

My boys are all football players. There isn't a game they come home from where some area of their body isn't bleeding from turf burn. We have a regular routine to keep the wound clean and help the healing process: spray some hydrogen peroxide (it's gonna sting, no way around it) followed by some antibiotic cream and a Band-Aid. After they shower, we let the wound get some air. Our goal is to work together to heal the wound as much as possible before they play their next game. If the wound doesn't heal, it will immediately rip open and begin bleeding on their first drive down the field.

The same is true for our emotional health. What we don't repair, we repeat. It takes honest self-reflection and willingness to lean in to the hard parts of life we just want to deny. Will you choose to nurse your internal scars and heal? You don't have to do it alone. I'm here to help walk you through this journey of hope and healing.

My life is marked by pretty scars. My healing is deep and redemptive. And yours can be too. Healing takes work, and you're capable. It's going to take a little more than hydrogen peroxide, antibiotic cream, and a Band-Aid, but it's also going to open life up in ways you never thought possible.

3

I Cussed a Lot

How Grief Can Taste Like Tears and Sound Like Swearing

Grief. It rears its ugly head when we least expect it. Sitting in the orthopedic office a few months after my divorce to receive a diagnosis of "tennis elbow" was unnerving for several reasons. First, I don't play tennis. And when I do try to join my kids on the tennis court, I really shouldn't. It's bad. Truly. I've played a handful of times, and each time I'm so terrible that I nearly pee my pants due to the laughter created from my weakly returned shots. Also, I use the phrase "returned shots" loosely because the balls rarely make it back over the net. Please note, I'm not overstating my atrocious tennis abilities. I'm that bad. I believe it's also important to note that I'm not at all competitive. I value laughter over winning, hence the number of times I'm doubled over laughing rather than celebrating my win on the court. Therefore, tennis elbow seemed like a bit of an erroneous diagnosis.

Grief snuck in before I even made my way back to be examined. In the course of filling out fifteen different pages of information as a new patient, I arrived at the blank "in case of emergency contact" line. I no longer had an in-case-of-emergency person. Whose name would I now write in that blank? I panicked. For twenty years, that blank had never stumped me. I would write my then-husband's name and his phone number—the only ten digits I had memorized other than my own—and move on to the next blank. But now I was divorced. When my husband left, I lost my in-case-of-emergency person.

My eyes filled with tears as the blank taunted me. My mind started bouncing around the lies that creep into your head after experiencing a failed marriage.

You're alone.

No one loves you.

Everyone in this waiting room knows he left you.

You'll die old and lonely.

I know this last one seems extreme, but at times our minds quickly jump to worst-case scenarios in a split second.

Hearing a nurse call my name snapped me back to reality as I wiped a solo tear and tried to explain I hadn't completed my paperwork yet.

Grief. It visits us in large and small ways, sometimes causing us to escape to our bed for the day, and other times as a looming blank line that taunts our tender hearts. And at other times it spews out as justified, yet often misunderstood, anger.

I chose a cortisone shot in the joint of my elbow to take away the pain. It hurt like the dickens, like childbirth pain only a much shorter length. It relieved the nagging ache in my elbow, gave an explanation for my teary eyes, and also created a distraction I needed from the abandonment my heart was feeling. If only there was a shot to relieve my grief. An easy way to mend my broken heart.

One of the hardest situations for me to accept was the division of time with my children. I wanted my kids in my house 100 percent of the time. It just didn't feel "fair" to have to share my kids every other weekend. Honestly, it created more agony for me than any other part of the divorce scenario.

And I had to relive it every other Thursday. Watching my kids get in their dad's car and drive away for four nights didn't get any easier. In those moments, I grieved. I grieved the loss of my family unit. I grieved four days without interacting with my boys. I grieved that my kids had to live this back-and-forth life. I grieved that they lived a life where they had to pack every other weekend. It was sad to hear them ask, "Whose weekend is it?" They were kids; they should only have to deal with one home.

Regularly that grief would overwhelm me, and the anger took over. Many of those Thursdays I stood where I could watch my kids crawl up into the car, watched the car back out of the driveway and head off down the street, and then slowly closed and locked my front door.

That's when the cussing would start. I'd yell and scream at the top of my lungs all the things I wanted to say. All the things that needed to come out and not be held in any longer. Words came out of my mouth that I'd never want my mother to hear me use. My emotions ranged from betrayal to devastation to longing. I felt the anguish of rejection deeply, and my kids leaving for the weekend just intensified those emotions. I felt like I hated him for what we were going through. I had a primal urge to hit or destroy something and vacillated between disbelief, hurt from the abandonment, and rage that this was the reality of my life. At the same time, I felt deeply vulnerable and exposed.

Sometimes I'd turn the anger on myself. Why had I enabled bad behavior? Why had I chosen to forgive his actions again and again? How could I have believed the lies that were spoken over me for so long? How could I not see the calculated manipulation that had been used to control me for so many years? Why had I fallen for it? How did I stay in a relationship that included so much betrayal?

Part of the grief process is grieving how you allowed yourself to be treated. Possibly feeling anger for the first time in a very long time about the negative behaviors you couldn't see at the time and the abusive situations you were put in. Letting the anger flow freely. Grieve that you were in a relationship where you weren't valued. Possibly you weren't seen or known or even really loved. Here you find yourself post-divorce, and you finally recognize and understand that you are worthy and deserving of so much more than you were ever given in your past relationship. You may recognize the neglect of your marriage and the dysfunction you lived in for far too long.

Grief isn't negative. Grief is natural. Grief is necessary. You must allow yourself to feel all the emotions it encompasses.

Grief feels like a black hole where there is no escape. Hope feels far away, and the anguish wrenches your soul. There are two extremes to watch for in grief. One is allowing your grief to overtake you, to become absorbed completely in your pain. The other is avoidance. It's easy to choose to become distracted by so many things that allow you to ignore the hurt you so desperately want to heal.

Writing quickly became my solace. It began in a really unexpected way. One afternoon, following a terrible counseling session where a lot of terrible things were said, I drove home and thought, *Who am I really? What is true about me?* And I grabbed a notebook off the bookcase, began furiously scribbling everything that was bouncing around in my soul, and gave it form on paper. Thoughts were no longer floating around in my head but released when my pencil hit the paper. Writing in my journal became a daily grounding practice for me. Writing was where I took the fuzziness I felt in my heart and clarified my emotions on paper. Writing was how I processed my grief and allowed all my disappointments to empty out of my head and onto the lines. Writing solidified what was next for me and allowed me to begin to dream for my life.

Writing helped me find my voice, and in finding my voice I began to recover my life and started the process of restoring my soul. I've never calculated how much money I've spent over the last six years at therapy, intensives, and other practices that guided my growth and helped me emotionally heal. What I will say is that I'd spend it all over again because it was worth every penny: No doubt it was all money well spent.

With that said, one major benefit of a regular writing practice is cost. Writing is a form of free emotional processing. It allows you to specifically dig into your emotions, dump out your thoughts (both conscious and once-subconscious), and clarify thought patterns to help you heal, and in doing so, you can begin to reclaim your life. My friend Allison Fallon says, "Words are everything, yet most of us are not using them to their fullest potential or to our greatest advantage. Words are the most powerful tool we have to create the life we long for. Yet they are often our most under-utilized resource."[1] Stream-of-consciousness writing in my journal gave me freedom. It clarified pathways of opportunity and desire.

Writing in a journal is a really simple activity. Almost too simple. But it opened a door where I began to grow from my grief and my anger. It was my safe place to say whatever needed to be said. Anger isn't an emotion I easily access. Writing allowed me to release the anger swirling inside me in a healthy, productive way. We often believe that our grief will shrink over time. I've learned that what actually happens is that we grow around our grief. Writing was my avenue to personal growth. It became a roadmap to the life I dreamed of creating for my boys and me. Freedom began to bloom in my life as my pencil poured out words onto the pages of my journal. There wasn't a formula or a daily expectation. It was stream-of-consciousness writing that allowed me to begin to uncover my new life. It grew my confidence and allowed me to actually strip away all that I thought I "needed" to be and remember and rediscover who I already was.

Writing is where I began to find healing and hope. It was in the pages of my journal that I first realized I would get through the divorce, start over with my boys, and be better than okay.

That day in the doctor's office, I couldn't write a husband's name in the space reserved for an emergency contact. But I learned how to see that God was writing a new story in me, and I saw it while sitting on an upholstered seat in a waiting room. The same is true for you: You can begin to see the new story God is writing in your life.

As you move forward one day at a time, invest in yourself and your healing. Go for a twenty-minute walk outside, allowing your mind to be distracted by nature and the beauty of the world around you. Buy yourself a beautiful journal and grab your favorite pen and use the practice of writing to help you begin to process all the emotions that are surfacing in your life. Meet a friend for coffee and make the choice to lean in to vulnerability and share how they can help you begin to move forward. Small, intentional daily acts can have a significant impact on your life, your perspective, and your sense of who you are. Love yourself enough to take the time to reflect on and process your grief and anger. Don't deny those emotions; embrace them in ways that heal and develop growth in you.

4

From Bent to Bold

How to Move from Brokenness to Bravery

The day I filed for divorce I hopped on a plane and flew to Nevada to help cohost a work event for the nonprofit that I'm employed with and have co-led for the last fifteen years. The event only happens once a year and is attended by more than a thousand female Christian leaders from all over the world. I'd hosted this event with my best friend for seven years, and we had developed a pretty natural rhythm together and seamlessly complemented each other on stage.

But this year I was walking out on stage knowing that not only was I no longer a pastor's wife, but very soon I would no longer be a wife.

As I grabbed the microphone to greet the ladies to kick off the event, the only people who knew that the end of my marriage was imminent were two of my best friends and my parents. I wasn't carrying a secret. I was privately processing the only choice I'd been given in regard to my marriage. Outwardly, I walked on stage standing straight, strong, and with a smile. Inwardly, I had been living life bent for far too long.

In Luke 13, Jesus heals a crippled woman—the Bible describes her as *bent*. This is another woman we don't know much about; we don't even know her name.

> One Sabbath day as Jesus was teaching in a synagogue, he saw a woman who had been crippled by an evil spirit. She had been bent double for eighteen years and was unable to stand up straight. When Jesus saw her, he called her over and said, "Dear woman, you are healed of your sickness!" Then he touched her, and instantly she could stand straight. How she praised God!
>
> Luke 13:10–13

If I had to guess, I'd bet this woman wasn't seeking attention at the front of the crowd. Eighteen years of crippling affliction had probably created some shame, shyness, and desire to avoid attention. That's a posture I understand. The unraveling of my marriage and subsequent divorce left me wanting to hide out and not be noticed. I remember days when I'd take the kids to school, come back home, park the car in my garage, quickly hit the button lowering the garage door, and retreat to my bedroom on the second floor, hoping no one would ring the doorbell for a visit—and if they did, I could easily pretend I wasn't home.

For this woman in the Bible, living life bent made maneuvering through life painfully difficult. Navigating streets and crowds all while having a singular view facing toward the ground had to be not only dangerous but also mentally challenging. This woman's view was always facing down. However, she'd chosen to enter the synagogue that day. Weaving through packed streets, busy crowds, and narrow stairs couldn't have been an easy task for a woman who walked bent. A moment with Jesus was worth her burdensome travel. While we may not know much about her, her faithfulness and inner strength speak volumes. She made bold decisions to navigate the difficult travel with a significant disability to seek healing. Her resilience and desire to be with Jesus changed her life.

I walked on stage that day at the conference knowing I had a lot in common with the bent woman. The realization that I'd been living my life bent was difficult to admit but also needed to be said out loud. During the month since the resignation from the church, through meetings with leadership and staff, in articles that had been written on blogs and Christian websites . . . I'd never chosen to use my voice. My focus had been on protecting my kids and just getting my bearings. For years I'd been hiding in the back, hoping not to get noticed. God had begun the process of healing me. On the outside I stood straight and tall, but my soul was ravaged and hunched over from the years of feeling betrayed, controlled, and manipulated.

In the Bible, in one moment of healing, the bent woman's perspective drastically shifts from viewing only the dirt to being able to see all of creation. Can you imagine? For eighteen years she'd only seen the ground; trash rolling around the streets, dusty feet in sandals, dirty animals as they passed by. And in a few seconds, the touch of her Savior and the words from His mouth completely healed her. She stood straight. She could look up to the heavens. Now she saw faces in awe of the miracle they were witnessing, she made eye contact with Jesus, and her viewpoint moved from seeing the stains of dirt to raising her eyes up in praise.

My healing took a lot longer than a few seconds to happen, but it happened all the same. It happened by slowly moving through my grief, and in doing so, I could see that I'd been living my life much like this woman. I lived my life bent, and that wasn't the life God wanted for me, nor the life I wanted for myself.

On a work trip a few years before my life imploded, I recognized that I felt most like myself when I wasn't around my then-husband. I could say what I was thinking, make the decisions I wanted, and respond authentically without correction, negative feedback, or criticism. When I was traveling with friends or working at Leading and Loving It, I'd feel this comfort in who I was and in what God had called me to. There were even a very few times I'd allow myself to imagine and ask myself, *When I'm eighty, will I look back on my life and regret staying in my marriage and allowing the disrespect, broken trust, manipulation, and lack of love and connection?*

After the divorce, my confidence was shattered, my self-esteem demolished, and I doubted God's ability to use me. Beginning to allow God to heal my heart meant slowly working to stand to see a different landscape—a landscape that displays glimpses of hope.

In a lot of ways, it began that day I walked out to greet those women. They all knew something was going on in my life. His resignation meant I was no longer the pastor's wife of Cross Point Church, and everything around that was perceived as "scandalous." This is the point where, standing beside me on that stage with a thousand pairs of eyes staring at me, my best friend, Lori, suggested we address the elephant in the room: me. Yes, I was the elephant in the room. People had heard of his resignation, but what that meant for the kids and for me was unknown. There I stood on stage, beside my best friend, with a massive pink elephant projected on the three screens around me, ready to begin stepping into this new path . . . AND I was afraid. Terrified, actually. As relieved as I felt, I also felt fear. The emotions coexisted.

Standing on that stage was hard. My heart pounded in my chest, and I was a shell of who I had been twelve months earlier—having quickly dropped forty pounds. I had some poorly written notes I'd scribbled on my flight in my right hand, but I knew I could do hard things. Sometimes even when we're doing hard things, we're doing it afraid. And that's okay. Doing it afraid is better than not doing it at all.

The dress I'd chosen for that day was selected with intention; I didn't want it magnified on stage how thin I'd gotten. The words I'd chosen seemed to just scratch the surface of all I was feeling. The reality was that there would be no turning back from this moment. There would be no more hiding and no more denying what was really happening in my life.

The silence in the room was deafening, and every eye was on me. I'd tried to prepare myself for what that moment would feel like, and I hadn't even come close. I'd expected the fear, the anxiety, the tightness in my jaw. I hadn't prepared myself for the love that filled that room. I wish every one of you reading this book could feel that love and support, could be empowered by those one thousand cheerleaders wanting the best for you and your future. Those ladies in the audience didn't need to know all the nitty-gritty details; they needed to know I was going to be okay. Their concern wasn't about what had happened but focused on how I chose to live my life moving forward.

I took a deep breath, secured the microphone one more time, and just inhaled the moment. As I've mentioned, at that point in my life, my days back in Nashville consisted of getting the kids to school and hiding out in my house. Here I stood on a stage in Vegas, declaring in front of an audience of one thousand women how I'd lived life bent for far too long, how I was okay, and how I believed that eventually I'd be better than okay. I acknowledged that God had never called me, or any of them, to live life bent, and I claimed that now that I'd begun to stand straight again, I'd embrace what God was providing in the midst of the loss. Even though that stage time felt like an eternity, it only lasted about five minutes—but they were possibly the most bold, brave, and empowering five minutes of my life.

As scary as that moment was, it also kickstarted a huge streak of growth for me because it allowed me to finally speak about what was going on in my life. So much of what had been going on had been hidden behind the scenes, but now was my time to speak truth. Creating congruence between my inner life and the outer representation built truth, and truth was something I'd been begging God to give me for months. I'd been asking for God to reveal truth, but I was realizing truth had been inside me all along.

I finally allowed myself to admit how terrible things had been in my marriage and acknowledged I'd permitted unhealthy actions and forgiven multiple betrayals. I didn't stand on the stage and air a bunch of dirty laundry. I was honest that I still had more questions than answers and had absolutely no clue what was next for me and my boys, but I had a voice, I was bold, and I was beginning to stand straight again. I told those women that the role and position I'd filled at Cross Point was gone, but no one could take away God's call on my life. The only reason I was still standing was because of God; the hits would keep coming, but He was calling me to stand straight and lock eyes with Him.

To begin this process of standing and healing, I first had to walk through the pain of my grief. I was forced to confront the death of the dreams I had for my family, my marriage, and my future. How do we embrace hope as we are trying to stand while grief engulfs our heart? How do we feel secure in the midst of inevitable uncertainty?

The last word had barely escaped my lips when the entire room stood to show their support of me. Tears fell down my face, and as I looked around the room, many of them had joined me with tears of their own. Since that day over six years ago, I've had the opportunity to speak to many of those women, and they echo how empowered they felt hearing me share. They use words like *brave* and *courageous*. Looking back, *brave* and *courageous* aren't words I'd use to describe the emotions I was feeling. Rarely do we feel brave in a moment of true transparency, but choosing transparency will be one of the bravest things you do.

After that day on the stage, "I am safe with Jesus" became the cry of my heart. Physically I'd felt safe, but emotionally and mentally I hadn't felt safe for years. The mood in the home kept me walking on eggshells and extremely cautious of my words and actions. I craved safety yet never felt it. "I am safe with Jesus" was the positive affirmation I repeated to myself over and over again each day as I walked ahead in this new season of life. I was walking through a divorce, but I felt safer than I had in years. My husband no longer lived in our home, but I felt safer living as the solo adult than I had living with a partner. It was a phrase I consistently tracked in my journal, a phrase that allowed me to begin to breathe again. Finding my safety in Jesus meant I learned to remain attentive, calm, and obedient, and I learned to trust my intuition. I was learning to trust myself again.

Standing on that stage gave me courage I didn't even know I would need later on. But that courage—given to me through those women in the audience and, of course, through my Savior—is what helped me to begin processing my trauma.

As I began processing my trauma, I believed that I had to move on from the grief completely, when in actuality, my grief was something I would choose to move forward with. Grief allows us to navigate life in healthier ways, to see beauty from ashes, and to recognize the sacred in simplicity. Choosing to feel my grief and all that was lost was a big part of what helped me begin to move from bent and broken to strong and straight. Allowing God and others to share that pain with me gave me a healthy posture. Isolation had kept me bent and fearful; sharing in my suffering began to straighten my outlook on life and give me glimpses of hope.

Being intentional with grief creates a life lived at a higher place of peace and understanding. We can never take our pain or our grief away. Instead, we just find a safe environment, a safe place, to experience our grief. Removal of grief isn't our goal; processing through it is. Finding context for the grief by connecting with others who have similar experiences or connecting to a cause related to the grief can be helpful. And often, a grieving person needs to be given permission to live again, to know it's okay to experience grief along with joy, to feel pain alongside hope, and to recognize that often our most heart-wrenching losses are also springboards for our largest leaps of growth.

Never would I have expected that standing on a stage at a conference was how I'd begin to use my voice again, but that moment of authentically sharing opened something in me that I couldn't contain. It didn't remove my grief, but it gave me the courage I needed to keep going. Doing it afraid made me realize that when I was back home and having a rough day, or often a rough week, I could get out of bed and keep going. The strength that moment in Vegas provided unleashed a desire in me to continue to stand straight, even when I was tempted to live life bent because it was familiar. Standing straight isn't always easy, but living life bent isn't really living at all.

I'll say it once again: Grief isn't negative. Grief is natural. Grief is necessary. I firmly believe there's a misconception when it comes to grief. We think our grief will shrink. That the more time passes, the smaller our grief will become. But our grief doesn't shrink. It stays the same. We are the ones who grow around grief. The grief is part of our story, and who we become is often because of that grief.

Time doesn't heal grief. Healing heals grief, and your healing will look different from others' healing. Time doesn't heal grief. It's your courage to deal with everything you used to avoid. It's your bravery to give attention to your pain and address all you've been bottling up. It's your dedication to working through the tension that has held you captive and kept you bent for far too long. Be patient, and don't compare your journey to others.

We all have to rebuild our lives during and after divorce differently. We each have different stories. We all bring different heartaches, different circumstances, different brokenness, different wounds, and different work into the rebuilding. One of the biggest gifts I was given as I walked through my grief was time. It's hard to watch someone you love grieve. Often, because we love them, we try to hurry them through their grief because we don't want to see them hurt and struggle. We do it because we love them, but it's not what's best for them. Everyone grieves at their own pace. It's a humble friend who realizes they can't hurry your healing. It's a humble friend who allows you the time you need and points you to Who you need.

There is a partnership with the work of the Holy Spirit in our healing. God working with us. God working in us. God working through us. It's both God and it's the Holy Spirit partnering in us for healing. Can God do it all on His own? Yes, but He desires for us to partner with Him. The beautiful partnership of us and the Holy Spirit—we don't work to earn that from God, but because He has given us new life, He is restoring us and we *get to* partner with Him. Link arms with Him in your grief to move forward and do the work of healing.

God allows us to partner with Him in really tangible ways. How does this all shake out practically? I can't restore myself. I can't heal myself. I can make circumstances look different, but at the end of the day, I don't want just an appearance of healing. I want to have walked through my grief, my desperation, my hurt, my anger, and to partner with God to live a life restored to His glory.

Here are some tangible ways you can work through your grief over your divorce, release yourself from living life bent, seek healing in your life with God, and begin to live life standing straight.

- Unpack trauma with a trained counselor
- Do things outside your comfort zone
- Have hard conversations
- Be patient with yourself
- Prioritize your needs
- See a therapist on a regular basis
- Replace unhealthy coping with habits that sustain your needs
- Develop a support system
- Allow yourself to process your feelings without self-judgment
- Strive for consistent contentment, not constant happiness
- Embrace a lot of self-compassion
- Accept setbacks as part of the journey

Moving from bent to bold and beautiful is a process. As we look back at the woman in Luke 13, we see the leaders of the synagogue were there to challenge Jesus in performing the miracle on the Sabbath. Luke tells us this:

But the Lord replied, "You hypocrites! Each of you works on the Sabbath day! Don't you untie your ox or your donkey from its stall on the Sabbath and lead it out for water? This dear woman, a daughter of Abraham, has been held in bondage by Satan for eighteen years. Isn't it right that she be released, even on the Sabbath?"

Luke 13:15–16

While studying the end of this passage, I kept focusing on the word *released*. Jesus states that the woman's healing *released* her. As you surrender the burdens, shame, pain, and grief you carry, you will be released. I don't believe you will be released of your grief—you will carry your grief with you and grow around it. And the woman you will become is strong and capable, resilient, bold, and healthy.

You'll be released as you partner with Him in your healing.

You will stand straight again.

Your period of living life bent is ending as you move to being better than okay.

5

Whose Voice Do You Hear?

How to Shake Off the Shame

L et's just do the ole one-two punch and knock out grief and shame back-to-back. The emotions related to grief and shame dance together closely during divorce. Shame regularly accesses your head and your heart. Shame that you're walking through a divorce. Shame that you have been left. Shame that you're not worthy of love. Shame that your marriage failed. Shame asks, "What's wrong with me?" Shame says, "I am broken." I can't tell you the number of times I've been at coffee with someone, and as they are telling me their story, their voice drops in volume, they hesitate slightly, and they whisper, "I'm divorced." Friendly reminder: Being divorced does not make you less important, less valuable, less desirable, less loveable, or second-class. Yet we often feel shame.

Even if you weren't the one who wanted the divorce, shame often enters the picture. Even if you remained faithful to your spouse, shame causes us to question our worth. Even if you fought hard for your marriage, shame has a way of creeping in and creating disgrace in our lives.

Research supports that self-compassion and kindness toward oneself through the divorce process is crucial to making the emotional experience more manageable.[1] In the midst of the grief and shame that assault our tender hearts, we're all seeking "more manageable" ways to find hope and healing.

Some of us are coming out of an unhealthy relationship that possibly involved verbal, emotional, and mental abuse. Due to the abuse, family-of-origin wounds, and efforts to function in a dysfunctional relationship, we battle negative thought patterns. I walked through years of being told untruths about myself. To my memory, a few of those negative, repeated phrases were . . .

You're too emotional.

You're irrational.

I have to go behind you and clean up the messes you create at work.

You shouldn't be upset about . . .

You're not a leader.

People only like you because of me.

You're a terrible time manager.

You probably have your own list. What I noticed over time was, even post-divorce, I continued to hear my ex-husband's voice in my head. There's a good chance you understand what I mean. As I moved forward with life and began to tackle new challenges and chase new dreams, I kept hearing the things he'd said to hold me back. His voice of negativity bounced around in my head more often than I wanted to admit.

I was living my life with shame that had been put on me by another individual. I'm guessing you have a similar story with someone in your life. Words that have been spoken over you that you believe. Words that crush your heart and remove your focus from Jesus. Actions that cause you to believe you're not worthy of love.

We may end up in relationships where someone projects their shame onto us. I believe I lived a lot of years carrying someone else's shame because they were too weak to deal with it.

Some of you are living your life with someone else's shame. Shame that was put on you. Shame that weighs you down. You're living a life of dishonor because someone else dishonored you. You are stuck in the rubble of the lies spoken over you, and you've allowed those lies to become the filter you experience life through. You hear a voice in your head whispering those lies.

Whose voice do you hear in your head?

The ex-husband who said he never loved you.
The parent who told you you'd never amount to anything.
The boss who said you weren't smart enough for that promotion.
The coach who told you that you didn't measure up.
The friend who said you were a disappointment.
The teacher who laughed at you in front of the class.
The best friend who betrayed you.

Whose voice do you hear in your head?

Let it be God's.
Let it be God's.

When that voice of insecurity and doubt creeps in, stop and ask yourself, *Whose voice do I hear?* Stop and recognize whose voice it is you're hearing, and shut that unhealthy voice down. Invite God's voice to be the voice you hear. Allow His voice to speak truth into your head and your heart.

I have several sticky notes hanging around my house that say, "Whose voice do I hear in my head? Let it be God's." Maybe you need to do the same. Or set an alert on your phone to remind you. Show yourself some self-compassion—remove the negativity and replace it with truth. Self-compassion is directly related to self-love. Practice giving yourself grace. It's time to shake off the weight of that shame. Give it to God, and allow Him to release you from the shame that holds you back. It's time to get past your past. To rebuild the parts of your life that shame destroyed and receive your double share of honor He promises.

God wants to repair the bruises of your heart.
He wants to restore the places in your soul long devastated by
    people who were supposed to love you.
God will renew the ruined dreams of your life that have been
    devastated.
He wants to raise a new life out of your wreckage.
He removes the weight of shame you've carried for years.
He wants to give you freedom from the dishonor that holds
    you down.

When I was a kid, my dad worked as a truck driver. He started his days a few hours before we were up and usually walked in the door in time for dinner in the evening. The first thing he always did after kissing my mom was head to their bedroom and empty his pockets. Blue jeans were his uniform, and by the end of his long days, both pockets were full. He'd usually stick his hand in one front pocket at a time and dump the contents on their bathroom vanity. Coins, a pocketknife, small pieces of trash, Chap-Stick, receipts, and a number of other random objects were sorted. The contents of his pockets represented a few things: what he'd started his day with, what he'd picked up along the way, and what he needed to get rid of. I imagine that he emptied his pockets f irst thing to feel lighter and to transition from work to home.

Let's think of our lives in correlation to my dad's pockets. There are a few things we begin life with: a family of origin, shelter, care providers, the necessities—kind of like his pocketknife and Chap-Stick. There are for sure a lot of things we pick up and carry along the way: self-confidence, understanding, mistakes—similar to his change, which was sorted each evening. Then there are the things we need to get rid of: harsh words, embarrassment, failures, criticism, doubt, feeling like a misfit, abuse, insults. This list could go on and on; this is where shame comes into play. This is the stuff we need to get rid of. What are you carrying in your proverbial pockets you need to get rid of? What do you need to dump on the counter and throw in the trash? What can you remove or shed that will make your life lighter?

We have to change the way we talk to ourselves if we want to cultivate true shame resilience. Personal narratives that are filled with shame keep us hidden and alone. Truth sets us free. You don't have to wait until a faulty shame script pops up in your head to correct it in love. You can proactively declare truth over yourself. Say these affirmations out loud:

I am enough.

I am allowed to have good things.

I can get better.

I am not defined by my past.

I deserve to be loved.

I don't have to hustle for my worth.

My body is good.

I am proud of myself.

I am allowed to be human.

I like who I am.

My emotions are not too much to handle.

I am worthy.

I am loved.

I am worthy of connection and belonging.

I am not a mistake.

I don't have to be perfect.

I deserve healthy relationships.

I deserve to be seen.

It's okay to be soft.

I am more than my worst day.

I am not too much.

I did the best I could.

What do you need to add to this list to replace the shame holding you back?

Jesus didn't just take on our sin and death on the cross. He took on our shame. Replace the shame in your life with God's truth. In doing so, you will begin to fully understand your own value. It's time to empty your pockets, shake off the shame, and get rid of what is weighing you down and holding you back. Embrace what is life-giving and shed the shame that has shackled you.

6

I've Never Missed My Ex

How Loneliness Both Hurts and Heals

've never missed my ex-husband.

But I've felt immensely lonely.

Loneliness is one of the most difficult emotions to process when your marriage ends. At times it can take your breath away and create a longing you don't know how to satisfy. It's a void that creeps in and brings you to your knees. Words like *shame, anxiety, emptiness, panic,* and *helplessness* are often used to describe loneliness. The concern is how we respond to the loneliness. Do we acknowledge it and take an active approach against it, or does it spiral us into deeper isolation?

I believe it's one of the worst parts of divorce. For me, it took some deep reflection and finally admitting to my therapist and to myself I'd been lonely in my marriage for a long time. I'd battled loneliness for years, but this new form of loneliness felt hopeless and like there wasn't an end in sight. At least before, there was the physical body of another adult present. Now it was just me. Loneliness isn't being alone. Loneliness is the feeling that no one cares.

Often, we don't miss our ex, we miss the illusion of who our ex was. Who they presented to everyone else. Maybe they weren't a pastor, like mine, but were respected in the community or well-known because of their position at work, but the person you lived with at home was different. They might have been kind to everyone else but not to you. They might have used words of praise for everyone else but had only insults and scorn for you. It's difficult when everyone else in your life is telling you how amazing your husband is and you know the truth of feeling his manipulation and angry control. You don't miss your ex—you miss who you wished he really was.

Loneliness is unfortunately inevitable. It isn't *if* it will come but *when* it will visit. The impacts of loneliness can affect you mentally as well as physically. Nathan Spreng, PhD; Danilo Bzdok, PhD; and their colleagues note, "A sense of loneliness has also been associated with health risks that are equivalent to or exceed that of obesity or smoking 15 cigarettes daily."[1]

At a country music benefit concert with a friend, I heard a lyric that gave me goosebumps and caught my breath. Living in a suburb of Nashville means you have to be a country music fan—or at least that's how I like to think about living close to the Country Music Capital. The reality is, I've been a country music fan my entire life. Yet never did I expect such a therapeutic message to come from a country song. In his song "Signed, Sober You," HARDY sings of *healing in the midst of the lonely*. I know those lyrics aren't just catchy, they're true, but in the process of healing, I must admit I loathed lonely. And I must also admit he's right. The lonely is where we can reflect and dig deep. Lonely is where we become comfortable with ourselves. For some of us, lonely is where we meet ourselves again for the first time in a very long time.

About a year post-divorce my therapist said to me, "I think you need to sit in your loneliness." Not the advice I wanted, but she's wise and I trust her, so slowly I learned to sit in my lonely. In the beginning, it was miserable and I shed tears, but I was able to find some healing in my lonely.

Initially I was lonely any time I was by myself and even sometimes when I was with people. Loneliness is tricky; at times we can be surrounded by people and yet still feel lonely. As I began to sit more in my lonely, I noticed I did well during the day, but as soon as the sun began to set, my anxiety kicked up and I could feel it coming on strong. It was so interesting how my body responded (we'll touch more on the body's responses to divorce in a later chapter), but as soon as it was dark outside, I seemed to settle a bit, my anxiety lessened, and I realized I could make it until bedtime.

The *anticipation* of the lonely was sometimes the worst part. My lonely is how I began to find myself again. Loneliness helped me realize I was going to be better than okay. It forced me to be comfortable with me. So many people never take the time to become comfortable with themselves and like themselves. Loneliness gave me permission to really take the time to reflect on who I was at the core and to articulate liking that person. As crazy as it might sound, loneliness was another stepping stone toward freedom. Let's look at some action steps to work through loneliness well.

Acknowledge the loneliness

The loneliness you're feeling is normal. For me, the loneliest times were Friday nights and Sundays. When I was married, Friday nights had always been a very social and fun night for us. We were usually with a group of friends and their kids enjoying dinner together followed by some super fun activity. Upon getting divorced, I wasn't sure where I fit. Being with all married couples was hard, yet I didn't feel the simple label *single* was the best fit for me either. Plus, my friend group changed drastically as my marriage fell apart.

The group I had previously spent so much time with no longer existed. Our community was built around other staff families, and due to the resignation, some of those families moved, left the church, or also resigned. And if the community had still existed, I'm not sure I would have felt comfortable engaging. The layers were being peeled back; the faces in the church had changed. I wasn't sure who my friends were.

On the Friday nights when my kids were gone, I began the tradition of my favorite sushi and a Netflix binge. As silly as it might sound, that small tradition gave me something to look forward to that I tried to enjoy on my own. On Saturday nights I always met a friend for dinner or a movie. They were small routines, but again, they gave me something to look forward to and, to be honest, in the beginning, a reason to shower and show up.

Fill your time with things you can savor

The house I lived in during my divorce was right across the street from the largest public park in Nashville. I can't tell you the number of hours I spent hiking the trails of that park. I'd pop my earphone in, turn on my favorite worship music, and hit the hills. Being in nature was a beautiful distraction for my aching heart. I felt close to God and spent large amounts of time pouring my heart out to Him as I walked. The physical exertion also helped improve my sleep. Loneliness would often visit as I lay in bed alone at night. I'd shared a bed with someone for twenty years, and a now-empty bed was a constant reminder of the reality of my new life.

This was also the season of life when I took up yoga. The practice of yoga was helpful for a few reasons. I almost always scheduled my yoga when I could meet a friend. It made me accountable to spend time with someone who cared about me as well as got me out of my house. Because I was new at yoga and learning the terminology, my mind stayed constantly engaged on what my body was doing instead of circulating fears and anxiety around my divorce. It was the only time my brain received a rest from the worry, anguish, and pain it was processing. The time on the mat was a true escape.

Allow yourself to feel loneliness in parenting

If you're a parent, I'm going to share about a loneliness that I still struggle with that you might face as well. The loneliness that currently visits and brings tears is loneliness as a parent. Co-parenting is challenging for me. I wish it could be different, but currently it can't. There are times when something significant is going on with one of my kids, and I feel lonely because I don't have the ability to celebrate my kid with their other parent. Maybe it's a graduation or they had a great performance in a game. I don't have the opportunity to lock eyes with their dad and just share this moment of pride. To acknowledge together, *He's a special kid.* It is a level of loneliness that feels like it will never end.

Loneliness can creep in during rough patches with my kids, when it feels like I'm the one doing all the disciplining, having the tough conversations, and enforcing the punishment. I'm carrying it all on my own. That's hard.

When those moments hit, I acknowledge they are hard. I usually call a single-mom friend and process the loneliness with her. I remind myself it isn't that I'm not loved or my kids aren't loved, it's that our family was broken, and this is some of the fallout. The good news is the loneliness of those moments is fleeting; I allow myself to feel it, acknowledge it, and then celebrate the heck out of my kid.

Recognize there is good in the lonely

On my most recent birthday, I woke up to an empty house and composed this journal entry:

> This weekend I entered my 47th year. If I'm honest, it feels a little too close to 50! And at the same time I see so much life in front of me.
>
> I woke up on my birthday to an empty and quiet house. And I was okay with it. Let me say that again. I was okay waking up to an empty house on my birthday. That's one thing I'm happy to say about myself, I'm okay being with me, I'm okay being alone. Just a couple of years ago, waking up alone on my birthday would have felt extremely lonely and cued immediate tears.
>
> But I've learned there's a huge difference between being alone and being lonely. And there are definitely worse things in life than being lonely.
>
> I've learned to appreciate my struggles, because without them I wouldn't have found my strength.
>
> I've learned starting over means trying to stand on shaky legs, but the rising again is what matters.
>
> I've learned that it doesn't matter how well you know the people in your life if you don't first know yourself.
>
> I've learned that living a full life involves growth, learning, grace, and self-awareness. And I trust the process of growth.
>
> I've learned that the greatest gifts in life are the people God places around you; I'm immensely grateful for those people.
>
> Here's to 47!

Consider a pet

Enter Maggie. If you could see me right now, you'd see me sitting in a leather chair with my laptop desk in the corner of my bedroom. Only, I don't sit in this chair alone. Maggie, my two-year-old pup, is always curled up beside me. Actually, she prefers to rest her head on my right forearm, but that makes it nearly impossible to type. I do regularly refer to her as my coauthor for this book as I talk out loud and process ideas and her ears perk up in curiosity at my words.

Christmas 2020 was a doozy. My oldest son had his second shoulder surgery a few days before the holiday, and it was also the pandemic . . . and he got COVID-19 at the surgery center. He was resting in my bed while the rest of the family celebrated Christmas in the living room. After spending about ten minutes checking on him and making sure he had everything he needed, I returned to the living room to find what I thought could only be a baby coyote wrapped in a pink blanket, sitting in my recliner. My kids had surprised me with a puppy. They were nineteen, sixteen, and fourteen at the time. It was such a thoughtful gift. It was a gift they wanted me to have so I wouldn't be alone when they were gone. This is where I should also add, we already had a dog. An eleven-year-old bird dog who was spoiled rotten, the most high-maintenance member of the family. Now we were a two-dog family.

Just what every mom wants: a gift she has to take care of for the next fifteen years! The pup was eight weeks old and the cutest baby coyote I'd ever seen. Maggie is a Texas Heeler, which means she's the most loyal dog ever. We quickly became inseparable. In fact, I'm certain she's the healthiest codependent relationship I've ever had.

A four-legged companion also provided an outlet for the physical touch I'd been missing. She curls up against my back at night and tucks herself in my lap every morning. I never walk into an empty home. She's there to greet me each time I walk in, and there hasn't been a single time she wasn't happy to see me. Taking on the responsibility and time commitment of a pet isn't for everyone, but I'd be remiss to not acknowledge the healing and happiness my Maggie has provided me.

Lean on God, who never leaves you lonely

Allowing loneliness to pull us closer to God instead of pushing Him away will allow us to see God in a way others can't see. When you're leaning on God, He opens your eyes to allow you to see beauty in your loneliness. It focuses our spiritual vision to recognize Him at work and share His faithfulness with everyone who crosses our path.

I'll tell you, when I was so desperate that all I had was God, I was able to see Him move in ways other people weren't able to see.

It probably comes as no surprise for you all to hear that my anxiety level shot way up during the last year of my marriage, and it hit an all-time high with a panic attack at a hotel during the trip to Vegas I mentioned earlier.

While I pretended like everything was okay, in reality it was crashing down around me. And when he left me alone in our hotel room that night, I thought I wouldn't make it through the darkness until morning. All I could do was lie in bed, weep, and recognize how lonely I was and that there was no relief in the foreseeable future.

It was earlier that day, while sitting by the pool, that I had heard his words that he had never really loved me. That he married me twenty years before out of guilt and obligation. I knew my marriage was in terrible shape. I strongly felt there was probably someone else impacting his decisions and words. I knew hope for my marriage was bleak. But that was the day I realized that my marriage was probably not salvageable.

I don't know how many of you have experienced a panic attack—they're terrifying. Your chest tightens, your breath shortens, your heart feels like it's coming out of your chest, your hands shake, your jaw locks up; it's frightening.

My best friend was ten minutes away, and I didn't call her. The shame, fear, and panic overwhelmed me.

We often use the phrase "I have no words," but that night, lying there lonely and alone in that hotel, I had just one word; I cried, "Jesus, Jesus, Jesus, Jesus," over and over. The name of Jesus was all I could mutter. I cried out to Jesus because I was alone. I cried out because of my pain and devastation. I cried out because of my immense fear.

And in my loneliness, heartache, devastation, panic, and suffering, I could feel Him with me. His presence was in that room providing comfort.

Don't miss the fact that the only word I said over and over was Jesus, because in my loneliness, I knew He was my lifeline.

In my loneliness, the whispering of His name was praise.
In my loneliness, repetition of His name provided safety.
In my loneliness, He was my constant companion.
In my loneliness, He was my hope.

The same is true for you.

In your loneliness . . . His name is praise.
In your loneliness . . . His name is worship.
In your loneliness . . . His name is prayer.
In your loneliness . . . He provides you safety.

In your loneliness . . . He is your constant companion.
In your loneliness . . . His name is HOPE.

There's not a lot I miss about that immensely lonely season in my life. But the closeness I felt with God was beautiful. To see Him at work in large and small ways in my life made me feel so loved, when the person who was supposed to love me the most left. The prayers I poured out to God in my journal included awe and affection I hadn't experienced before. The intimacy of it being just "God and Brandi" during so many moments in the midst of my loneliness was beautiful. That was the reward for my faithfulness that I never expected.

I still have desires in my life that haven't been met. I desired for God to bring me the right person to love quickly. That hasn't happened . . . yet. Don't get me wrong—I have a full life, I enjoy my mom life and parenting my boys, and we have a great rhythm to our family. My job is stimulating, allows space for my personal growth, and is very fulfilling. I'm grateful for the life I live. But there was a season when the desire for companionship was a longing that could accompany moments of hopelessness.

My prayer during that season was repeatedly asking God to remove the longing, to take away the deep desire I had for a relationship. To allow that desire for love with a partner to fade just enough that I lean in and trust His timing with my love life. To help me feel complete as I am, with Him as my constant companion. It was a hard prayer to pray because I know at my core I'm created for companionship, and part of me wondered if by praying this prayer I was admitting I could be single forever and not experience a marriage companionship again. And at the same time, I never doubted that God could remove the longing of my heart in order to allow my focus to be on companionship with Him first and foremost.

I survived that lonely season, and I came out stronger.

I'm emotionally more resilient than I was six years ago.

God uses me in so many more ways than He did before my divorce.

God has strengthened my relationships with my friends and my family.

He has given me a closeness with my boys that brings me immense fulfillment and joy.

I have been to hell and back, and I'm still standing and ready for what's next.

This is what I want you to hear. You might be going through hell right now, but you're going to be okay. You really are. Just take one day at a time. God is still going to use you. You will survive your divorce and the loneliness and come out stronger. He's going to give you strength to see you through.

Don't miss what God has for you, right where you are in your loneliness. He dwells in you and knows you in an intimate way. You might feel lonely, but He is with you during those long, dark, and panic-stricken nights, at your kids' sporting events when you might sit alone, and on holidays when you don't have your kids. He is all you need and desires to fulfill your deepest longing. He is relentlessly pursuing you.

I want you to know that loneliness gets easier and, dare I say, learning to embrace loneliness and getting comfortable being alone may be something you come to enjoy.

Last weekend I did something that might sound crazy to some of y'all. I spent the weekend at home alone. By choice. Just me and the dogs. AND I was okay. In fact, I thrived.

Things had been going one hundred miles an hour, and my introverted soul was drained. Empty. On zero. Zilch. The boys were gone, and I had nothing on my schedule. The empty calendar brought me a ridiculous dose of anticipation.

A few things to note . . .

- Four years ago, a weekend alone would have had me in tears
- I'm about 50/50 extrovert/introvert
- I was never lonely during the weekend
- To make my weekend alone happen, I responded *no* to a couple of invitations and didn't have FOMO

I journaled how I spent those days to help me remember the value of feeding my soul. When I worked on updating my budget and finishing some emails, I had the organizing show *The Home Edit* on in the background, and in the evening I'd chill to one of my favorites, *The Marvelous Mrs. Maisel*. I completed simple tasks like reorganizing my bathroom, roaming aimlessly through Target, or having a two-hour catch-up phone call with a friend. I reveled in being alone in my house, something that seemed foreign to me just a few years ago.

I want you to hear that I'm sorry for the loneliness you're battling. Please know that I know and battled those same emotions. As you sit in your lonely, I pray you find healing, you find strength, and most important, you find yourself.

Humbly Grateful or Grumbly Hateful

How Gratitude Is a Game Changer

Choosing a gratitude mindset is the simplest step I took that made the largest impact on how I viewed my life daily during the end of my marriage, and has continued still today. In fact, it's almost so simple that setting aside an entire chapter to talk about just gratitude seems a little silly. Trust me, it's a game changer in how you process what you're walking through, how your focus shifts, and the perspective with which you see your future. The deeper you have experienced pain, the greater capacity you have for joy. And the bridge between pain and joy is gratitude.

There is a slew of research supporting links between gratitude and happiness as well as gratitude and resilience. But it doesn't stop there: Even the medical community is aware of the correlation between gratitude and our health. A large study conducted by Virginia Commonwealth University showed that thankfulness predicted a significantly lower risk of major depression, generalized anxiety disorder, phobia, nicotine dependence, alcohol dependence, and drug abuse.[1] If that doesn't convince you, then maybe this will: Studies have found that giving thanks and counting blessings can help people sleep better, lower stress, and improve interpersonal relationships.[2] Who doesn't need better sleep and lower stress? Gratitude is a game changer.

A few months into my divorce, a question I'd used on my kids when they were younger kept bouncing around in my head: *Am I humbly grateful or grumbly hateful?* At that point, I knew I had a decision to make, one that would guide my heart to freedom or lead me on the pathway to bitterness. In my heart and in my head, I took a stand and told myself, *God is still good, I know He is. Nothing around me feels good or hopeful, but I know God is still good.* That's the incredible thing about gratitude; you can choose it even when you don't feel it.

That same day, I chose to make a point of seeing the good things around me. I pulled down an empty journal that had sat on my bookshelf for years, grabbed an orange Sharpie, and wrote "Focus on the Good" on the cover. Some days my list would be more serious and list areas of growth, steps toward emotional health, and moments with God I wanted to forever remember. Other days it included simple gratitude, like indulging in ice cream on the porch with my kids, practicing a new pose in yoga, or meeting a girlfriend for a margarita.

Author Melody Beattie says, "Gratitude unlocks the fullness of life. It turns what we have into enough, and more. It turns denial into acceptance, chaos to order, confusion to clarity. It can turn a meal into a feast, a house into a home, a stranger into a friend."[3]

And for me, it did. It allowed me to step outside my pain and see God at work in my life in large and small ways. To focus on gratitude allows us to realize how blessed we are even in the midst of heartache. Seeing how God is still working and doing good in our lives keeps us from being crushed by tragedy and despair during seasons of life when we feel uncertain.

Adopting a gratitude mindset is something everyone is capable of. I have always described myself as a glass-half-full gal, so gratitude was easy for me to practice. However, if you're more glass half empty, this is a simple step you can take to help you survive your divorce and come out stronger! Gratitude isn't ignoring reality. It involves self-reflection and self-awareness. The intention of seeing life as it is and still finding ways to be grateful.

Gratitude leads to happiness

The practice of positive psychology lists gratitude as one of the five building blocks of happiness. Gratitude is a choice you make. You can look at each day and ask yourself a few reflection questions:

- What might be a more helpful way to look at this situation?
- What are you most grateful for today? Why?
- What good do you want to come of this?
- What are you telling yourself in the heat of the moment? Is it helping or harming you?

That last question might be the most important in terms of personal growth. It's a shift in how you're viewing yourself, the message you're allowing to bounce around in your head. Gratitude is something you can choose because it isn't an emotion. Gratitude is a posture.

Gratitude reminds you of His power

No one wants to walk through life alone, especially on the bad days. What initially began my gratitude practice was knowing that God was still good regardless of my life feeling so bad. In the midst of divorce, disappointment, and devastation, don't we all want a little good infusion? Finding ways to record seeing His goodness in your daily life allows you to remember life is bigger than the situation you're walking through. It helps you remember that He's got you.

> Don't worry about anything; instead, pray about everything. Tell God what you need, and thank him for all he has done. Then you will experience God's peace, which exceeds anything we can understand. His peace will guard your hearts and minds as you live in Christ Jesus. And now, dear brothers and sisters, one final thing. Fix your thoughts on what is true, and honorable, and right, and pure, and lovely, and admirable. Think about things that are excellent and worthy of praise.
>
> Philippians 4:6–8

This passage of Scripture has been a bedrock for me since college. A few things strike me about this well-known passage. First, Paul is writing from prison. Yes, he's in prison reminding the Philippians not to worry about anything. From behind bars, Paul has set the example by telling God what he needs and thanking Him for all He has done, which produces peace.

We're promised peace when we show God gratitude. Paul then ends with the reminder to fix our thoughts on what is true, honorable, right, pure, lovely, and admirable.

Gratitude allows you to focus on the present and feel thankful

That's right. As much as we want to jump ahead and get through our pain—spoiler alert—that isn't how life works, at least not a life where you want to heal from your hurt. When walking through a divorce, you have more bad days than good. The days are long, and the finish line seems unattainable.

Gratitude forces you to be present and also find something to be thankful for. I remember one particularly dark day when my gratitude list included my new hair dryer. Yep, I was grasping for good on that day. Is a hair dryer life changing? Probably not. Does a hair dryer point to God? Ummmm, that feels like a stretch.

Listing my hair dryer was a present reminder that there would be new, and not just new hair devices. There would be new memories made, new relationships formed, new laughter filling my home, and new hobbies to enjoy.

Recently I heard Dr. Robi Sonderegger, an internationally recognized clinical psychologist, speak on the five character traits necessary to grow through trauma. Dr. Robi stated that through his clinical work, research, and consulting with survivors of war, human trafficking, and natural disasters, he'd observed that a gratitude practice can help create growth as you heal from trauma. And just because I know you're curious about the other four traits, they are hope, faith, kindness, and courage.[4]

Gratitude shifts perspective and changes how you live your life. It begins with small shifts and grows into a lifestyle. It allows you to view your life by seeing what's there rather than what isn't.

A large part of writing this book has been going through my journals from the last six years. I've revisited the details of the dismantling of my family in very raw and real details. I've waded through the simplest of gratitude lists and the prayer requests that seemed impossible at the time.

You may be shocked to hear that I read journal entries from the worst period of my life, and I find myself grateful—grateful that I recorded daily life in the middle of walking through the end of my marriage. I look back and see my growth. I see strength and truth. I see small and large ways God loved me. Now I realize I was able to see the beautiful in the ordinary because I chose to focus on the good in my life. I knew then that even though life felt anything but good, God was still good, and God was still good to me. The same is true for you. God is still good, and God is still good to you.

I don't know what you're walking through today, but take a few minutes a day to focus on the good in your life. Reflect on your day and jot down four or five things that you identify as good. From sunshine to yummy coffee to long hikes to favorite songs to small personal growth. Record it. Write it down. Acknowledge there is still good in your life. Six years down the road, you'll be grateful you did.

Out of his Shadow

How to Step into Your Sunlight

was forty-two when life as I knew it ended and I had to figure out my life again. Starting over at forty-two wasn't something I'd ever envisioned or expected. At that point in my life, all my kids were in school, and one could drive. Before, forty-two meant finally being able to take some time and exhale after the busyness of parenting small children. It meant getting extra one-on-one time with my husband. It meant finally diving into *me* and revisiting my past career and what that might entail for my future.

But here I was, forty-two and single. Not just single, but divorced and basically alone. To be quite honest, I felt lost. Life as I knew it for decades had vanished. I went from being surrounded by thousands of people, leading a church I loved, to basically disappearing into my house and seeing only my therapist and very, very, very few friends. Describing it that way sounds pretty lonely and hopeless. The Brandi Wilson I had been for my entire adult life no longer existed. I just wanted to be an ostrich and stick my head in the sand and come back up when life had gotten back to normal. Moving forward meant I had to work hard to recognize myself in the midst of so much trauma.

There's a quote from the 1999 movie *The Talented Mr. Ripley* that Jennifer Garner reprised in 2016 during a *Vanity Fair* interview about her divorce. When asked about her marriage, she responded, "'When his sun shines on you, you feel it.' But when the sun is shining elsewhere, it's cold. He can cast quite a shadow."[5] I understood living life in the shadow of someone else. Her quote put words to the life I had lived for many years. And now that shadow was gone. He was gone. I'd grown so used to the shadow that had been cast over my life that I'd stopped paying attention to who I was outside of the dimness of his shade. Life felt shaky, but I loved the warmness of the sun that now shined on my face.

I remember being a little girl and pretending I could change my name. I wanted to be Nicole. Nicole felt so fancy and glamorous, and Brandi felt so plain and small-town. In my mind, Nicole was very stylish, had the most beautiful bedroom a little girl could dream of, rode a bike with purple streamers from each handle, and did not have a freckle on her entire body. In fact, I loved the name Nicole so much that I even went through the official process of getting a new birth certificate for my Cabbage Patch doll so at least that bald preemie could live out my new-name dreams.

As a little girl, pretending to have a new name was fun and exciting. As an adult woman knowing you're in the middle of a crisis that will redefine you, a new name is frightening and even paralyzing at times.

My friend pastor Chris Nichols once told me, "It's one thing to be given a new name. It's another thing to walk in it."

My past identity had been wife, pastor's wife, church leader, church planter, supporter, and chief encourager to the staff, and all of that was gone.

One of the most well-known stories in the Bible of being given a new name is found in Matthew 16 when Jesus speaks to Peter. Peter was a man of great faith, and also a man of great inconsistency. The story of Peter beautifully illustrates that while it's one thing to be given a new identity, it's something else entirely to walk in it.

> Jesus replied, "You are blessed, Simon son of John, because my Father in heaven has revealed this to you. You did not learn this from any human being. Now I say to you that you are Peter (which means 'rock'), and upon this rock I will build my church, and all the powers of hell will not conquer it. And I will give you the keys of the Kingdom of Heaven."
>
> Matthew 16:17–19

Whoa, that is empowering! Jesus tells Peter, formerly Simon, his new name means *Rock*—not the former wrestler turned actor, but rather a symbolic anchor for the church. *Rock* brings forth thoughts like solid, foundational, stable, and sturdy. As I said earlier, Peter was a man of great faith, and also a man of great inconsistencies. Because it's one thing to be given a new identity; it's another thing to live it daily.

After all, Peter is the disciple who lost his faith and sank when walking on water toward Jesus. Peter is also famously known for denying Christ three times. At one point when Peter was trying to get Jesus to turn away from His suffering on the cross, Christ responded, "Get behind me, Satan!" (Matthew 16:23 NIV). Yep, Peter, whose name signified he would be an anchor for the church, also didn't get it right all the time.

One thing I knew about my new life was I wanted it to represent the change God was making in me. I was no longer in an unhealthy relationship and could be fully Brandi.

Moving forward was overwhelming. I was starting over in every aspect of life. Now I was a single mom starting a new career and purchasing a home on my own, and I was the sole financial provider for my family. Add in all the decisions, changes, and unknowns! I was overwhelmed. There was only one way to move forward in my new identity—one day at a time.

When life is turned upside down and looking toward the future brings on total panic, remember your goal is to make it through today. There will come a time to plan for the future. To be excited about all that is in store. To dream about what is to come. But to be a real woman in the midst of hard times, your goal is to make it through one day at a time.

One day at a time. Make the decisions you have to make today. Deal with the problems you have to face today. Have the conversations you have to have today. Celebrate the little victories you have today. Life isn't lived in the past or dreamed about in the future. Life is lived in the today.

A second thing I learned about moving forward in a new identity is to recognize what God is teaching you in the minor moments. The one thing God was teaching me in the minor moments that surprised me most was freedom. I believed I was free. I live in an affluent city in America, the land of the free and home of the brave. I have great health care, a beautiful home, and a pantry full of food. Compared to some of the experiences I've had on mission trips and various volunteer opportunities, I thought I was free. I viewed freedom as personal independence, as the ability to make choices.

But I wasn't living the life of freedom God had dreamed for me. I was so attuned to meeting others' needs and living life alongside someone else that I had lost the freedom Jesus had given me.

It's often the minor moments in the midst of heartache that teach me the most. A couple of years post-divorce I was getting ready to go to one of my regular yoga classes, and when I walked into my closet, a necklace that a humanitarian organization I regularly worked with, World Help, had given me caught my eye. The gold square charm had been stamped with the word *freedom*, representing the work World Help does to stop sex trafficking across the globe. But it represented so much more to me personally. I had worn that necklace on days when I knew I needed a strong reminder to choose freedom. When I touched it on my neck, I would say a little prayer, thanking God for the freedom He was showing me. And that morning I put on the necklace, declaring freedom for myself.

Honestly, I thought to myself, *I don't wear jewelry to yoga, it gets annoying and in the way. Why am I putting this on today? I haven't worn it in a few weeks.* But because I am always running late, I pushed those thoughts aside and headed out the door. I walked into the room to a new instructor, a lady I had seen around the studio but didn't personally know. And as she started class that morning, she went to a vulnerable place and acknowledged that she was in a terrible season of life. Things were falling apart, but the mindset she was choosing was freedom from the pain, freedom from the disappointment, and freedom from the heartbreak. At that moment I knew I hadn't worn that necklace for me but for her. After class I approached her and introduced myself and passed on the necklace. Tears sprang to her eyes, and we had the most beautiful conversation.

That minor interaction with her reminded me that being real and walking in my new identity means I need to share what God is teaching me. I need to recognize that God will use my pain to help someone else. I need to share how He brought me through the fires. It's about letting others know they aren't alone in their struggles; that's one way I can help make this world a better place.

Jesus gives us new names and new identities. My heartbreak was public, it was embarrassing and humiliating, and I experienced human rejection at one of the greatest levels. From the guy who brought the groceries to my car at Kroger, to the kid behind the counter at Subway, to the couple who I sat beside on a flight, it seemed like everyone I crossed paths with knew what I had walked through. On more than one occasion I'd hear people address me or refer to me as Pastor so-and-so's ex-wife. That phrase created instant nausea. But I always responded gently and reminded them, "I'm Brandi Wilson."

For a couple of reasons, I'd chosen to keep my married name. First, it matched my kids', and I didn't want any more confusion for them. Second, it was how I'd been known my entire adult life, and I didn't want the confusion of changing it. I've been asked why I didn't go back to my maiden name many times. For me, I wanted my new family unit to match and be cohesive. I have a couple of friends who did go back to their maiden names and love it. Do what feels right for you. No one is walking this path for you, so do what feels like the best fit for your future. My human nature wants to hide that ugly piece of life. But God doesn't just give me a new name; He calls me to walk in it.

When I examine my life, I realize God was using minor moments all the time to remind me how He loves me in big and small ways, and of the importance of sharing my story with others, whether in conversations, small interactions, or someone seeking me out. I have to choose to hold my head high and share how He has rescued me. To remind other women that a husband might leave you but God never will. To show others that even though titles and positions might be taken from you, God gives your calling, and only He can take it away. To share with others I am His daughter, I am an overcomer. I am strong. I am a leader with a powerful testimony.

Often in situations where life is turned upside down, we desire a quick fix, instant healing, the immediate gratification of forward momentum. In reality, stepping into a new identity and walking in the truth of who you are is a process, and it involves a lot of waiting. We're not waiting on God, we're waiting on our acceptance of what has happened in our life and our belief of what God has in store for us.

Wait for the LORD; be strong and take heart and wait for the LORD.

Psalm 27:14 NIV

Waiting on the Lord brings a calmness and clarity we can't obtain on our own. It creates a peace in knowing we aren't in control; we actually don't have the weight of the world on our shoulders. Learning to walk in my new name meant I stopped and took time to just exhale and remember to be strong and wait, because my God is faithful.

One spring, I went through a really horrible joint counseling session with my then-husband. I won't get into the details, but I left the office feeling like my character had been maliciously and falsely assailed. It was so hurtful. I climbed into my well-worn Honda, laid my head on the steering wheel, and wept. The tears streamed down my face; I was gutted and broken and didn't know what was next.

Yet with those tears came a moment of clarity. I experienced a transparent recognition of MY Truth—not the hurtful things I'd heard but *Whose* I was and the character, integrity, and heart He'd created in me. I clearly remember lifting my head and saying out loud, "Those things are NOT true, they're not who I am, he doesn't even know me." As soon as those words left my lips, I backed my car out of the parking space, drove directly home, and pulled out a notebook I had been using to take notes during counseling sessions. At the top of the page I wrote, "What is TRUE about me," and the list began to flow.

What is true about me—I am . . .

- Grounded
- Focused on what's best for my kids
- Caring
- Hardworking
- Thoughtful
- Self-aware
- Emotionally stable
- A deep feeler
- Sensitive
- Focused on the good
- Generous
- Witty
- Liked by the people around me
- Honest
- Truthful
- Aware of others' needs

Little did I know this list would become my first journal entry that would lead to thousands of entries where I poured out my heart and my hurt. I would go on to fill multiple journals, where every page documented healing and growth in my life. That moment was my first taste of freedom, and it would spur me forward into a hunger for more that I couldn't contain. That bit of freedom helped me see that so much more was to come; it helped me know in my core that my best days were ahead. I had been given a new name, and I had taken the first step in walking in it, chin up and head held high.

If you want to embrace the identity that God has for you in this new season of life, please take time to remember what is true about yourself. We are given a lot of messages in relationships. We're told who we are by our parents, coaches, siblings, teachers, bosses, friends, and just about anyone else we interact with on a regular basis. A lot of these relationships are healthy, and we receive messages of love and appreciation. Walking in your new identity means embracing what you know to be true about you.

Working toward a life of freedom was what began to drain out my fears. I had to lean in to the rediscovery of personal identity, as I was starting over in every sense of the word. It's yet another area of my life where I was constantly reminding myself to trust the process of healing and growth.

A tattoo I have offers the perfect illustration for this long process of healing. About a year before our separation, my husband and I went with friends to get tattoos. I had picked out my *Love More* tattoo, as it's a personal life motto. After many hours, all six of us were inked, and my now-ex-husband and I chose to put coordinating arrows on our ring fingers. It wasn't a tattoo I necessarily wanted, but my marriage was already feeling pretty rocky and unstable, and I was willing to do anything to show my devotion and dedication to him and to our marriage.

Fast forward twelve months; I'm separated and heading to a divorce. Looking down at the tattoo on my ring finger was brutal. It taunted me all day, every day, and reminded me I'd been left. So I began the long and expensive process to have it removed. But it wasn't happening nearly as quickly as I would have liked. I tried covering it with Band-Aids and masking it with makeup.

As it slowly faded, I realized that the removal process had to be reframed in my mind. The process was slow and would take time—a couple of years, in fact—and so would my healing. I wanted a quick fix, but stepping out of the shadow, allowing the sun to shine on my face, and stepping into a new identity takes time. The further into your skin's dermis the ink has settled, the harder the removal process is. The wounds I was healing from were deep and jagged, and they left a large impact; the recovery would be intensive and exhausting, but I also couldn't think of anything I deserved more.

It was a beautiful season, because as overwhelming as every aspect of life seemed, I felt more myself than I had in years. And most important, I realized I liked the person I was becoming. Brandi was pretty fabulous. The shadow I had lived in didn't extinguish my light—I had only been shaded, and the shadow had only brought gloom.

Spring is my favorite season for a few reasons. Flowers are blooming, the gray of winter is finally dissipating, and the sun's rays bring a long-awaited warmth. Every spring I find myself looking up, admiring the perfect blue sky, fluffy white clouds, and bright green leaves. Often I've described that as my favorite color palette. The warmth of the sun creates that clarity and provides that perfection.

The shadow of winter is bleak and dreary. Springtime light is bright and hopeful. As you move forward out of the shadow and into you again, I want you to remember your light was only shadowed. It wasn't extinguished, because you wouldn't allow it to be extinguished. You are a fighter. You kept going through the bleak and dreary. Life felt dismal, but you're in the light. You're strong, capable, worthy, loving, kind, and interesting. God created you to be unique, beautiful, and contagious. Look up and let the sun shine on your gorgeous face. Your future is bright and hopeful.

You shine.

My "Ex-Husband Knots"

How to Engage in
Self-Care and Soul-Care

An area that can't be ignored is how a divorce physically impacts your body. We talk a lot about the emotional and mental weight, but what my body went through without any conscious actions on my part was alarming. At the time I think I believed I was holding it all together the best I could, but my body's response to the severe agony I was walking through blew any appearance of being okay. Looking back now, this makes total sense to me. Our bodies are continually assessing the information around us and working hard to try to figure out how to keep us safe.

One of the suggestions my therapist made early on was to get regular massages. She knew that physical touch is a pathway of love for me, and receiving regular touch was something my head and my heart needed. I asked around and found an excellent massage therapist at a well-known local location and immediately made an appointment for ninety minutes of bliss. She was very thorough at her job; at my initial visit, she spent the first ten minutes asking questions about what was going on in my life and where I felt the stress in my body (btw, that's an excellent question to ask yourself: Where do you feel stress in your body?). In the course of conversation, I mentioned I was walking through a brutal divorce.

The knots in my shoulder blades took the majority of her time that first visit. She methodically yet gently worked until she could get them to loosen a bit. Lying there, I knew her work meant I might finally be relaxed enough to get a full night's sleep that evening. With such success, I booked a follow-up appointment for two weeks later. I walked into the following appointment excited to continue to get some release in my shoulders and couldn't help but laugh when the first question my attentive massage therapist asked was, "How are the ex-husband knots in your shoulders?"

Divorce takes its toll on your body, from weight loss to insomnia to mobility issues to depression. The body feels the impact of trauma. Emotional trauma impacts the body, and physical trauma impacts us emotionally. Our body's tissues and cells store our entire life story. In fact, research shows that our bodies store more than our brains, and events in our lives become embodied as they occur.[1] Therefore, if you don't integrate your body into your healing, then you are able to experience only a fraction of the total healing you need. Integration of the body is necessary because the cells in our body have no sense of past, present, or future. Our bodies immediately recognize a circumstance as familiar, and our conscious thinking has to catch up.

For instance, that's why we feel anxiety first in our body. Our heart beats rapidly, and maybe the jaw tightens or we begin to sweat profusely. One of the biggest lessons I learned was what self-care looks like for me. I began my self-care journey by learning to ask myself four important questions:

- What can I control?
- What isn't mine to control?
- What do I want?
- What do I need?

Self-care is often simplified to nice chocolates, nail appointments, and massages, but self-care is really about creating a life you don't want to escape from. In reality, self-care shouldn't impact only our bodies or only our minds but integrate the two. It's important to figure out what self-care looks like for you. Besides regular therapy, my self-care centered around three main areas: mindful movement, writing, and meditation.

Before we dig in to those three areas, let me give clarity to the importance of regular time with a qualified and talented therapist who is a good fit with you. Often when I ask someone if they have regular time with a capable therapist, they respond, "Therapy is so expensive." I would concur; therapy is expensive. However, not taking the time to pursue wholeness—and instead living in brokenness—will cost you more, literally and figuratively.

Choosing not to sit down with a professional who will help you identify your unhealthy patterns in relationships and establish healthy pathways will cost you more down the road. Working with a counselor to develop healthy coping strategies will save you money and heartache in the long run. I also understand you might have had a bad experience with a therapist. Likewise, I've had a nasty meal at a restaurant. But that nasty meal doesn't mean I stopped eating out, it just means I didn't visit that restaurant again.

Having a bad experience with a therapist doesn't mean you quit therapy altogether; it means you find a therapist who is a better fit. Now I'll officially step off my quality-therapy-is-of-immeasurable-value soapbox.

Mindful movement

You might be asking, what is mindful movement? Mindful movement is focusing your attention on noticing and feeling what your body does while engaging in movement. It's a mind-body focus where you become aware of your entire body, the places in your body you feel stress, anxiety, and worry, and learn how to release and relieve those types of emotions.

Mindful movement brought the responsibility of healing back to me, creating self-awareness as well as self-compassion. After a particularly difficult yoga class, when all I wanted to do was crawl into a ball and go to sleep, one of my favorite instructors shared this yoga mantra: "From a place of strength, we open. From groundedness, we offer our hearts. From stability, we expand." That mantra really spoke to me in regard to my own self-care. What could I do to create strength, groundedness, and stability in my life? These questions helped me start moving toward caring for myself more thoughtfully. The connection between mind and body created a congruence with myself that I had desired for years.

Another thing I learned on the mat was to breathe again. Obviously, I'm typing away at this book, so I've been breathing. But truly inhaling and exhaling was something I'd forgotten how to do. I felt like I'd lived a lot of life holding my breath. Cleansing breaths ground you and allow you to decrease the stress and increase the calm you're experiencing.

This connectedness to body might sound a little hokey to you at first, but in order for real healing and change to occur, the body must learn that it is safe so that you can function in the present.

Writing

As I mentioned previously, writing became my favorite way of processing my hurt, my wins, my steps both forward and backward. It was so valuable to my processing and healing that I'm reminding you once again of the benefits of writing. Similar to how the body metabolizes food, stream-of-consciousness writing gave me the ability to break down the events of my life. Nothing sees into the depths of a soul like writing does. Writing was like a mirror to my soul, a reflection of what I was feeling, and combined with gratitude, it helped me rewrite scenarios in my brain.

For years I had been a verbal processor, and still am, but writing was the conversation I needed to have with myself in order to recognize how I was feeling before I had conversations with trusted friends. My journals allowed me to dump negativity or doubt that raced in my mind. The self-empowerment and decisiveness that resulted as I wrote drew me back to opening my journal and grabbing a pen every morning.

Meditation

The third piece of self-care was the practice of meditation guided by Scripture, positive affirmations, and prayers that calm both the mind and the body. My brain is always full and bouncing around thoughts and ideas as soon as I open my eyes most mornings. In the midst of my divorce, my brain functioned in overdrive. Guided meditation allowed me to ground my thinking in something bigger than self, as well as process at a more manageable rate and make sense of what felt like chaos in my head.

Positive affirmations became a large part of that meditation time. Our bodies are addicted to the chemical cocktail when we think negative thoughts. The point of positive affirmations isn't to change our external world but to change the cocktail of chemicals in our internal world, which in turn affects our external world.

The Body Keeps the Score is a wealth of understanding in regard to our brain, mind, and body connection when healing from trauma. Bessel van der Kolk says, "Trauma results in a fundamental reorganization of the way mind and brain manage perceptions. It changes not only how we think and what we think about, but also our very capacity to think. For real change to take place, the body needs to learn that the danger has passed and live in the reality of the present."[2] Taking care of yourself and truly healing have to include your brain, mind, and body. It's imperative for you to work toward allowing your body to release the hurt it's carrying.

Van der Kolk goes on to say that "trauma and abandonment disconnect people from their body as a source of pleasure and comfort. . . . When we cannot rely on our body to signal safety or warning and instead feel chronically overwhelmed by physical stirrings, we lose the capacity to feel at home in our own skin and, by extension, in the world. As long as their map of the world is based on trauma, abuse and neglect, people are likely to seek shortcuts to oblivion."[3] Taking care of your self isn't a luxury; it's a necessity to your healing and growth.

Self-care isn't self-indulgent or selfish, and it's not one size fits all. Understanding what you need to regenerate and restore is important. It might take some trial and error. It could involve some experimentation. And that's okay. As women, we often spend so much time taking care of others well, we forget to take care of ourselves.

Here are some ideas of what self-care could look like:

- Setting boundaries
- Trusting your gut
- Eating a healthy meal
- Being kind to yourself
- Letting go of what you can't control
- Not giving in to people-pleasing
- Loving yourself
- Avoiding drama
- Ignoring negativity
- Writing in a journal
- Saying what you mean and meaning what you say
- Shutting down negative self-talk
- Dreaming
- Not being afraid to say "yes"
- Not being afraid to say "no"
- Avoiding numbing
- Going for a walk
- Taking a nap
- Enjoying the sunlight
- Spending time with friends
- Moving your body

Expand your definition of self-care and take some time to listen to your body: It's full of wisdom and wants to tell you what it needs.

Opening our hearts, dealing with the tears, acknowledging our pain—it's hard work. At some point in every healing journey there is a choice: We can either focus on what we have lost or pay attention to what we still have. In order to move forward, we must tame our triggers. This self-awareness work isn't for the weak. Taming triggers means we must come face-to-face with wounds and scars that may have existed for decades.

Triggers impact many of the interactions we have, and they can be both positive and negative. We've all smelled the delicious scent of goodies in the oven and been transported back to being a kid in our grandma's kitchen. On the other hand, we've probably heard a phrase or felt criticized and experienced an adverse reaction. A trigger is your body's way of telling you there is a deeper issue at play.

When the COVID-19 quarantine occurred, I found myself angry and frustrated. My three teenage sons were handling all the dramatic changes like champs, but I was anxious, frantic, and furious with the regulations being handed out. Protecting my family was of the utmost importance, but I couldn't get over the angst my body was feeling. A conversation with a trusted friend reminded me that the last time I'd lived life at this level of isolation was during my separation and divorce, when I was cut off from life as I had known it. Essentially, I was experiencing a very real and terrifying trigger.

The isolation I experienced during my separation and divorce felt cruel and deceptive. The isolation I was experiencing during the pandemic was born out of love and protection, taking care of those I love and keeping them healthy.

I felt almost immediate relief being able to identify what was triggering my emotion. But in order to process it, I had to do some inner investigating. Triggers can teach you and heal you. Triggers can also keep you stuck if you don't spend the time identifying and dealing with the cause and the response. Emotional triggers give us an opportunity to see what we're not looking at directly.

When you get triggered, get curious. You're being invited to go deeper, and by going deeper and doing some of that inner investigating, you'll be able to limit the emotional impact of negative triggers. Our entire life story is stored in our cells and body tissue. In order to properly access and work through those memories, our healing must be integrated. Working toward healing is often when we realize our light hasn't been extinguished, we've just spent too much time in the shadows of others.

A valuable part of self-care can also be reclaiming memories. Reclaiming a memory is revisiting a scenario, location, or situation that has a negative connotation for you and creating a new, positive experience to replace the old. It helps us reimagine triggers and allows us to create new memories. Taking back my power and control meant I wasn't going to stop going places because there was hurt associated with them. I refused to let the past decide where I would eat, vacation, or visit.

In the midst of my divorce, I was having a conversation with my best friend, Lori, telling her I was avoiding certain places and situations due to painful memories. She simply responded, "Well, we need to create a new memory around that." I immediately adopted her suggestion.

Over the course of the last few years, I have looked at situations and locations with more of a "I need to create a new memory" or "What is this place trying to teach me?" attitude, which has brought such healing and anticipation. It might sound crazy to say I ask what a place is trying to teach me, but avoiding a favorite ice-cream shop or restaurant because of an ex—that's a lot crazier.

I've already told you the *Love More* tattoo on my right wrist is my personal motto, but the memory behind getting that tattoo contains rejection, hurt, and disappointment. Some of the details around the day I got that tattoo can still unsettle me; however,

I'd never considered reclaiming the memory of getting my first tattoo.

I haven't shared much about my boys yet, but my oldest son, Jett, has always been one to know exactly what he wants and make it happen. It should come as no surprise that on his eighteenth birthday he had scheduled an appointment for his first tattoo. That's why one warm Saturday in May a few years back, I found myself sitting in a tattoo parlor with my oldest son, his friends, my other two boys, and one of my mom friends, watching my son and one of his close friends both acquire tattoos.

During moments of laughter and wincing, I realized, *This is a new memory!* Revisiting a tattoo parlor wasn't a memory I had planned to reclaim, and honestly one I didn't foresee needing, but it provided so much healing for my heart. In fact, that same day is when I got my next tattoo, a simple cross, to signify where my strength had come from. Coincidentally, my son also got a cross, but don't worry, they are definitely NOT matching tattoos. Because obviously, matching mother-son tattoos would reach a level of embarrassment that would classify as mortifying.

When you're reclaiming an old, hurtful memory, there are a few things you can do to help prepare your mind and your body. Notice what your body is feeling and name it. Is it anxiety or fear? Maybe you're feeling anticipation. Recognize where in your body you are feeling the emotion and acknowledge that. Get present, and remind yourself you're not in the past or the future, you are here now. Look around the restaurant, home, or event space and notice where you are—take in what's around you. Engage your senses and do some deep breathing. Deep breathing will help lower your anxiety and allow you to more easily reframe the moment.

Traveling on the weekends I didn't have my kids became something I looked forward to and greatly enjoyed as another form of self-care. It helped fill up my abundance of alone time and usually meant I was spending time with friends, people who loved me. I've mentioned one of my best friends, Lori Wilhite, a few times throughout this book. She lives on the West Coast, and the freedom to visit her more often was something I cherished. The time together involved laughter and an escape from my reality back in Tennessee.

But all trips must come to an end, and as my time away began to wrap up each visit, my anxiety would begin to rise. I knew I was heading home to an empty house and leaving my best friend. I felt safe with her and her husband, and even though I missed my kids and couldn't wait to see them, leaving her was hard. The number of times I crawled in an Uber or boarded a plane with tears streaming down my face are too numerous to count.

Finally, I started preparing my body and my mind about twenty-four hours before leaving. I'd acknowledge when the anxiety crept in instead of stuffing it. I'd sink into being present in the moment rather than jumping ahead. I'd become super vigilant about remembering everything about that time together so I could revisit it in my mind once I was back home. And I'd always make sure we had another visit planned so I'd know how long I'd have to go before being with her again.

I'm not sure where you find yourself today or what you are avoiding because of a past pain, but I challenge you to work hard at engaging your mind and body to create new memories. Replace that old hurt with new hope. Replace those tears with joy. Replace your sadness with a smile. Allow your body and your brain to work together so that *you* become a safe place for yourself.

"I Googled Dad"

How to Cling to Hope
When Your Kids Are Heartbroken

L eading the kids through the tragedy of divorce while just trying to make it out of bed each morning was incredibly overwhelming. The depression felt like more than I could handle
on most days. Parenting doesn't go away during trauma, so how
do we take care of ourselves and continue to raise our children?
Divorce generates emotional turbulence for the entire family, but
for kids it can be scary, anxiety inducing, frustrating, and confusing.

While spending some time at Onsite, a therapy intensive outside of Nashville, I heard a well-respected therapist, Bill Lokey, say,
"Your child's emotional resilience is based on their parents' ability
to own their own story, understand their story, and communicate
their story."[1] How I handle my healing during and after the divorce
directly impacts my kids and how they process emotional trauma
in their future.

Hearing how my healing would directly impact my children was pivotal. I knew there was value in pursuing healing for both myself and my children, but now I had the words to guide my journey. Often the best way we can take care of our children is to be willing to do the hard work ourselves.

To get to being better than okay, we have to do the hard work of building emotional resiliency for ourselves. Figuring out unhealthy patterns, why we have them, and how to correct them. Leaning in to our emotional health as we process what we've walked through and how it impacted our head and heart, then sharing that process with others.

Prayers for my boys filled the pages of my journal. I prayed God would draw them close and parent them in the ways I might be lacking. I begged God to protect their hearts toward Him and the church. I spent a lot of time asking for courage and the right words for tough conversations. I prayed God would guide my motives and actions as I walked through the divorce, not my anger, bitterness, or frustration.

One of the things that made my divorce difficult was that it was played out publicly. Blog posts were written, articles were penned, gossip abounded, and unfortunately my kids were old enough to read and understand a lot of it. That reality accompanied a load of embarrassment for them. I was wiping off the kitchen table one night after dinner when one of my sons doing homework from my desk close by said, "Have you ever Googled yourself?" I froze in my spot and inhaled deeply; I knew where this discussion was going.

He went on to describe how in the computer lab that day during free time, he and all his friends were Googling their names, their siblings' names, and their parents' names. He continued by telling me what he'd read about our divorce online, and what was information he already knew and what was information that was new to him. He went on to tell me how embarrassed he was by what had been written and how he hoped his friends never saw it. It was a hard and heartbreaking conversation, but one we needed to have, because the conversation gave me the opportunity to share some age-appropriate truth.

Communicate age-appropriate truth

Truth is a necessary part of walking your kids through divorce. I'm going to say something I can't stress enough. Regardless of whether you think you're keeping your kids protected by whispering on the phone with a friend or waiting until after they've gone to bed to have a discussion, or even maybe if you and your soon-to-be-ex are still living together, trying to navigate around one another and act like everything is "fine," kids know something in the home is off. They might not know all the details, but they know enough to pick up on the dissension and tension in their home.

Being able to communicate age-appropriate truths in ways that help heal their hearts as well as answer their hard questions is key. Often when kids aren't given age-appropriate truth, they create their own "truth" to make sense of the situation. Their "truth" almost always places them or something they have done as the cause of the end of their parents' marriage. How sad is that? When kids aren't given age-appropriate truth, they can begin to blame themselves when their parents' marriage ends.

Picture age-appropriate truth as a suitcase. Kids who are older can carry a larger suitcase and can usually handle more truth. Younger children might carry a backpack rather than a suitcase, and the truth they can handle is going to be much smaller. The level of detail of truth that is appropriate is based on their development.

Having a conversation with your kids about divorce isn't a one-size-fits-all discussion. That's why age-appropriate truth is so important. What does that mean? It means doing some research and learning what your kid is developmentally able to comprehend. One place to start is Nicole Smith's breakdown of age-appropriate communication for each developmental group in her article "What to Say (and Not to Say) to Your Children in a Divorce."[2] Remember, all kids are different, and some are emotionally more mature, so the recommendations are just guidelines.

Affirm your child's feelings

The top rule of divorce is to avoid talking negatively about the other parent. I totally agree with that strategy. However, I also think affirming what your kids are feeling and seeing is also of vital importance. You don't want their feelings to be ignored or discarded. That doesn't mean you trash the other parent—please don't put your kids in that scenario. But if you came out of a relationship and your ex isn't healthy and communication patterns were abusive, that disrespect and disregard can end up drifting down to your children. Let's look at a couple of examples.

If your child feels like the other parent repeatedly lies, instead of directly stating, "Your dad is a liar," one approach you could take would be to affirm their feelings and interactions by saying, "Your dad has an inability to tell the truth." Same information, different delivery. It affirms what your child is experiencing but doesn't use harsh language.

Maybe your child feels like the other parent isn't hearing them or their desires. You could help them process what they are feeling with "I understand your dad is hard to communicate with, and I'm sorry. I understand because he was difficult for me to communicate with during our marriage." That is a different response than, "Your dad is an incredibly selfish individual."

Kids will ask questions, and they will see things. Let them lead the process when they are ready. Respond with honest answers in a nonderogatory way. Honest, but not rude. If we sugarcoat conversations, our children won't trust us. Don't go into all the dirty details, but be honest with them. They can sniff out dishonesty. They need affirmation of their emotions. They're learning to trust their intuition. Your honesty needs to come from a place of healing, not with the motive of getting a jab in about your ex.

Post a calendar

One of the best tools I purchased for my kids was a huge three-hundred-sixty-five-day calendar. I placed it on the side of our fridge and carefully went through the entire year, marking holidays, spring break, and weekends. Kids like to know what to expect, what's coming next. Hanging a calendar helps them feel more independent and in control of their time. They're able to figure out where they will be which weekend, spring break, or holiday without having to ask.

Once my kids were older and all used digital calendars, I transferred it to our family online calendar. Then as they were making plans or leaving a practice, they knew who they needed to communicate with or where they were having dinner that evening. Having a visual representation of their time is empowering for children.

Respond to your children's father, not your ex-husband

Work hard to separate the roles of ex-husband and your kids' father. I know they're the same person, but the separation of roles can help guide your communication and help you see them with a different perspective in your reaction and responses. The balance it takes as a single parent to separate who your ex is to you and who that same person is as the parent to your children is not an easy feat. However, it's one I encourage you to lean into. When discussing parenting topics, have the conversation with your kids' dad, not your ex-husband.

There are times I've specifically had to remind myself I'm responding to my kids' father, not my ex-husband. In my mind, it clarifies our roles and guides how I choose to respond to choices or words that feel hurtful. In times when communication might be difficult or somewhat heated, the separation allows me to avoid taking a defensive position and to remain more neutral, keeping the focus on what is best for the kids.

Parenting as a single mom can be overwhelming at times. Being the only adult in your home carries a lot of weight. I'm the type of person who loves clear boundaries, detailed instructions, and distinct expectations. I'm quite literal. When I find myself in a difficult life situation where there are no instructions and zero positive expectations, I decide my job is to shoulder it all. Me, one person. I treat myself like I'm supposed to handle every worry, every problem, and every concern—and somehow I'm sure everything going wrong is my fault. I always think to myself I *should* be doing more. I *should* be over my hurt. I *should* be further along now. I *should* know what to do and not doubt my decision.

Where I carry this the heaviest is as a mom.

———

I love parenting. I love that I am a mom to boys. I honestly find parenting teenagers to be a lot of fun. But if I'm not careful, I can start to slide into a tendency of parenting out of fear. Anyone else know what I'm talking about? It doesn't take long for me to come up with a long list of things I don't want for my kids:

- ○ I don't want them to do drugs.
- ○ I don't want them to resent me.
- ○ I don't want them to mimic an unhealthy marriage.
- ○ I don't want them to not trust the Church.
- ○ I don't want them to stray from God.

I erect these walls of "protection" on the foundation of fear, and while these walls of protection feel justified, they block me from seeing the fullness of the vision God has for my family. One day I was reading in Joshua 3, about the ark of the covenant:

> So when the people broke camp to cross the Jordan, the priests carrying the ark of the covenant went ahead of them. Now the Jordan is at flood stage all during harvest. Yet as soon as the priests who carried the ark reached the Jordan and their feet touched the water's edge, the water from upstream stopped flowing. It piled up in a heap a great distance away . . . so the people crossed over. . . . The priests who carried the ark of the covenant of the LORD stopped in the middle of the Jordan and stood on dry ground, while all Israel passed by until the whole nation had completed the crossing on dry ground.
>
> Joshua 3:14–17 NIV

Let's break this passage down a little further. We're told the Jordan River was at flood stage, so likely double its normal width. Think one end of a football field to the other, from one yellow goal post to the opposite yellow goal post. Yep, I'm a total boy mom throwing in sports references like it's my job. The Jordan wasn't narrow, and it wasn't shallow. As the children's Bible song likes to remind us, it was truly deep and wide.

I love how the Bible says the water of the Jordan piled up "in a heap." I hear the word *heap*, and like all moms, I immediately have a visual of a heap of laundry. There's a constant heap lurking in my laundry room at all times to taunt me as I walk by. This heap was way more than a pile of dirty laundry; it was a barrier of protection.

This passage was so perfect for me in recognizing how I was parenting. For so long I thought leading my kids through tragedy and trauma meant walking ahead of them through the "Jordan" and that:

I had to carry the ark of the covenant on my own.

I had to lead them across the Jordan on my own.

I had to hold back the water on my own.

I had to present God's truth on my own.

I had to deliver them to the Promised Land on my own.

And I was terrified I was going to get it all wrong. I was scared to death the one thing I truly loved and wanted to get right—my boys—I would ruin because the weight of it all was so heavy.

Honestly, sitting on my couch that morning, I saw this passage so differently from the many other times I'd previously read it. That day I read this passage of Scripture and felt God telling me, "Brandi, that's not your job with your boys, you don't have to do it all on your own. You're not alone."

In reality, what God has called me to is to stand on solid ground and hold His truth for my family.

To stand on solid ground and hold God's legacy.

To stand on solid ground and hold God's inheritance.

To stand on solid ground and love His kingdom.

My job is to stand in the middle of the Jordan on dry ground and trust God will hold back the waters.

Trust God will be their barrier.
Trust God will be their protection.
Trust that God will lead my kids to His promises in their lives.
Trust that God will deliver them safely to the other side of tragedy.

I don't have to hold back the waters.
It's not my job.
At that moment, I knew that even though I was a single mom, I wasn't parenting alone. Sitting on that couch, tears ran down my face and I raised my hands in praise. I wasn't parenting alone. God was showing up in ways I'd never expected. The new understanding of this passage was such a beautiful reminder that He loves my boys as much, even more, than I do. The same is true in your life. You might be a single mom, but you aren't parenting alone. God loves your kids more than you can even imagine. It's His job to carry them to the other side of the tragedy of their parents' divorce.

Parenting during and after a divorce can take its toll on your heart. Wanting to be a healthy example of processing pain and walking through grief for your kids is something that you must make a priority. Watching your kids process their own pain is difficult. But I believe it's what's healthiest for them. As my favorite Fearless Mom Julie Richard has reminded me many times, instead of teaching our kids to *avoid* loss, we're showing them how to *manage* loss. That's a life lesson they can take with them forever.

11

Us Four, No More

How to Redefine Your Family for the Future

I know not every woman reading this book is a parent, so feel free to skip this chapter if you wish. But many of you are. And for those of you who are moms, the question I hear most often is, "Will my kids be okay?" It's a fear that looms near the surface, and one we personally want to do everything we can to rectify. As parents, the impact that our divorce could have on our precious children keeps us up at night and weighs heavy on our hearts. I looked for voices of wisdom to help guide me.

Finding a great therapist to help your kid process the divorce at their level of development is something I found to be of great value. Our family therapist helped us know what needed to be communicated to the boys and how to do so. He was also a wealth of information in regard to questions I had about being a single mom, co-parenting, and just boys in general. My home no longer had an adult male in it, and I soaked up any guidance and feedback about how to best parent my boys.

Allow friends to guide you

A few voices of wisdom I didn't realize I needed were friends who grew up as children from divorced families. I can't tell you the number of times I felt like I was making the best/healthiest/least-confrontational decision for my kids and then, upon sharing what I was thinking with one of my girlfriends who grew up in a divorced home, her gentle feedback would course-correct my thought process. Engaging adult children of divorce to help you process your parenting is invaluable. I don't know what it feels like to be a child caught in the middle of divorce, so consulting a friend who lived a similar story to my children was one of the smartest things I could do.

There are two specific friends I have leaned on for this feedback. I wish I could say it was my ingenious parenting that pushed me to seek the advice of these two friends. But having conversations with them about being a child of divorce, learning how it impacted them, and seeking their guidance in my parenting was totally accidental.

The first discussion happened during a quick neighborhood walk with one of these friends. We were walking and talking about daily life, and I began verbally processing an event that was coming up and explaining the reasoning for what I thought I was going to do. She waited until I was done and then asked if she could share how she thought my kids might feel. Her perspective on how my kids might feel because of the divorce opened my eyes.

I tell my kids often, "I've never done this before, this is my first time to do this too; I'm doing the best I can and figuring it out as we go." That's how I often feel navigating situations that feel tricky as a single mom. I didn't grow up in a divorced home, so I don't know how my kids feel and can't comprehend some of their struggles. I try to make the best decisions for them, but since I don't have the experience of divorce as a child, I truly have never done this before. I let them know I am doing the best I can and learning and growing along the way. Consulting friends whose stories are similar to the lives my kids are living has been incredibly eye opening and helpful. There have been a couple of decisions I've changed my opinions on because my friends weighed in on how it could impact my kids or how my kids might be processing the situation.

Redefine your family unit

The identifier "single mom" was initially terrifying to me. When I had children, I never expected to be the only adult in my household. Now, more than six years later, I've embraced being a single mom. The boys and I have a great rhythm and function well as a unit. One of my biggest fears as a single mom was redefining our "family." How do you move forward as a family and not feel like something is missing? When you've always envisioned your family unit with two parents, what does it look like to move forward and start over as a single parent? Working to redefine our family unit became my focus.

Parenting through trauma seems like one of the hardest things I've done. To be able to manage and process my emotions as well as give space for their emotions is a lot for someone who is a feeler. Part of surviving and starting over was to create a tight, safe nest. Our nest needed to feel very secure. We moved into a new home, and my number-one goal was for our home to feel safe and secure for our family.

So many relationships had changed in our lives that the number of people I engaged with shrunk as well. That meant the adults my kids came into contact with were people who had shown up for me during those dark days. I only engaged with people who I knew loved us and wanted the best for us.

As time passed and we began to heal, I slowly began to loosen the nest. Keep in mind, I thought my kids weren't aware of how tight I kept our nest. I thought they hadn't picked up on the fact that I was one protective momma bird. Then, in a conversation with one of my sons, we were discussing a new friend who was coming to dinner again, and he said, "I hope she realizes it's a big deal we let her into our family." In that moment I knew not only did they recognize I kept a tight, safe nest, but they appreciated and also needed the safety and security it provided.

Define your family values

Redefining our new family unit meant I spent a lot of time assessing what we value, what's important to us as a family. There were four values I wanted to focus on: laughter, time together, truth, and safety.

There had been enough tears shed—we needed to laugh together. One of my sons has impeccable delivery of funny one-liners, and his timing is perfection. Best of all, it's natural: None of it is planned. We've spent many nights around the dinner table just laughing at his humor. Working some funny television shows into our regular routine also brought a lightness to our home (*Ted Lasso*, anyone?). We each have a playfulness to our personalities that comes through in gentle teasing of one another and family inside jokes. Currently, everyone spends a lot of time mocking my laugh. Which means they've heard it a lot over the years, which also means I have succeeded with that value.

I also stole a phrase from a dear friend and parenting guru Julie Richard: Us Four, No More. One of the things I have loved about being a single mom is how many of my kids' friends we have in our home. Our doors are always open, and the snack pantry over-floweth. I've often joked that Jesus multiples our snacks like the fish and loaves, because I have no clue how I've afforded the numerous snacks and drinks over the years. Our house is lovely, cozy, and very lived in. But sometimes it needs to be just us. That's when I use the Us Four, No More terminology.

For instance, if we're doing a family dinner out to celebrate some event or special date, I'll say, "Let's leave for dinner at six; this is an Us Four, No More meal," meaning that I want some time just the four of us to catch up and chat. It doesn't even mean we're discussing anything major. It just means there will be a pocket of time when it's just the four of us together. I usually prefer Us Four, No More vacations, a chunk of time away together where we make memories and bond. It creates a focus on our family unit and helps solidify our relationships as individuals and as a family.

The house we live in represents a lot for me. One of the most important qualities it possesses is truth. There had been so much lying and deceit in our old lives, I made a strong decision that I wouldn't allow any of us to live in that again. My kids know truth is a high value for me and lying isn't tolerated. It took some figur-ing out, some tough conversations, and some arguments over the years, but I can proudly say we live in a house of truth.

My divorce forced me to recognize that I'd lived many years not feeling emotionally safe. I walked on eggshells in our previous family unit. Starting over and finding the peace of emotional safety was something I cherished and wanted to make sure my kids also experienced. Our family is emotionally, mentally, and physically safe. Some of us are more emotional than others, and those emo-tions are respected. It isn't always easy to share how we might feel, but we give space for that.

Create new traditions

Something that we've implemented is to regularly open our home to the boys' friends and share our addiction to milkshakes—hence, Milkshake Mondays. Every Monday night we have dinner at about 6:30 for whoever shows up. The table is *always* full and so is my heart.

After dinner and cleanup we move to the family room for quality television together: something from *The Bachelor* franchise. Yep, we pull out bean bags and blankets and everyone finds a spot. I like to joke that I use the trashy television show to teach how NOT to date (I feel pretty confident my publisher won't be asking me to write any parenting books after this admission). It seems silly, but there's always lots of giggles, side comments, and memories made. As the show is winding down, I pull out the blender and make milkshakes for everyone.

Milkshakes actually started in the middle of the divorce when I was trying to think of something fun for the terrible evenings we were living through. Milkshakes were something that was repeatedly listed in my gratitude journal because everyone loved them, and they were usually accompanied by a smile. I had no idea that making milkshakes all those years ago to get a simple smile would grow into a family tradition where my kids would invite their friends. It's one of my most beloved traditions that followed us from the past into the present and has allowed so many others to experience the safety of our home and family.

Now it is your turn

You have the opportunity to put the pieces of your family back together. Take some time and reflect on what your family values are. It's the perfect way to start rebuilding. Family values are just that: what you want your family to value. You can think of them as the glue that holds your family together. Envision sitting around the table on holidays with your adult children. What are the stories they'll tell? I feel confident a few contestants from *The Bachelor* will come up at our holiday dinners. But I also hope they tell stories of truth being told and of feeling safe to share their struggles.

Here are a few questions to ask yourself and your kids as you're determining your family values.

- How do you want people to feel in your home?
- How do you like to spend time together and time apart?
- What qualities do you value in other families?
- How do you want to describe your family?
- What do you want to guide your decisions, actions, and choices?

In *The Upside of Stress*, psychologist and educator Kelly Mc-Gonigal says, "It turns out that writing about your values is one of the most effective psychological interventions ever studied. In the short term, writing about personal values makes people feel more powerful, in control, proud, and strong. It also makes them feel more loving, connected, and empathetic toward others. It increases pain tolerance, enhances self-control, and reduces unhelpful rumination after a stressful experience."[1]

Creating family values will give framework to your new family unit. If you're feeling lost as a single parent, defining family values is a great place to start. It also helps give your children some ownership in their new family.

So, what does this chapter look like in actuality with my family now, six years post-divorce? God gave me a pretty sweet glimpse of all He's done while we were on our last family vacation. We've always been intentional to try to get away to the beach as a family. It's a week away from our regular rhythms of life to make some memories and just soak in time together. We do what we want to do, no agenda, no major plans—only penciled-in ideas and several fishing poles. Typically I'm not much of a selfie girl, but I snapped a selfie on our family vacation a couple of summers ago to remember the moment of embodied joy and to savor the fullness of my life. The completeness of my Us Four, No More family.

I've been a single mom for quite a while now; my boys spend the large majority of their time in my home, and I'm here to tell you we have redefined family beautifully.

A few things we do . . . we're intentional. We show up. We stay. We're truthful. Our family is safe. We trust one another. Our home is full. We have conflict . . . and we work it out. We have hard conversations. We love. We laugh. We make lots of milkshakes. We snap lots of photos. We cheer one another on. We fight over the bathroom. We work hard to allow the others to be their own individual and also a part of this incredible "fam," as one of my boys calls it.

My left forearm now sports a delicate tattoo symbolizing what the boys and I rebuilt. It has four whimsical stars that are lightly connected with "Us 4" in the center. It's a reminder of how far we have come and what family means to us. All four of us did the hard work together to redefine family, and my tattoo is a reminder of our dedication to one another and our family unit.

We're messy and beautiful together. We're family, and nothing's missing.

12

I Have a Six Pack and I Don't Mean My Abs

How Friendship Forges Strength

This book was born out of talking to so many women going through a divorce. Or friends, family members, or coworkers who had friends going through a divorce. Whether it be through referrals from friends, social media connections, or people from my past reaching out, I've had the opportunity to talk to a lot of women and a few men about the end of their marriage.

The first thing I usually start with is, "Tell me about your support system." It seems like a broad area to initially ask about. Most people expect me to ask more about what ended the marriage or where they are in the divorce process or how the kids are doing.

But the reality is, outside of their relationship with God, a support system is vital in hope and healing. Isolation can be detrimental. And trust me, I've done both. I've cut off communication and detached because the pain was too great. I secluded myself due to the embarrassment of failure. Coming out of feeling verbally and mentally abused in a relationship takes a lot of relearning. Relearning how to share the reality, relearning how to trust your intuition, relearning how to be vulnerable, relearning what it feels like to feel safe with another person.

In the early stages of my marriage ending, I wrote in my journal . . .

> I love my friends and my community, but I find it hard to engage right now because I feel so fake knowing how troubled things are at home. When someone says, "How are you?" I want to tell them, but I can't. The words won't come. So I pray and I write. God, show me how to not avoid friends. How to grow myself so I can share my burden and pain.

Leaning in to community isn't always easy. I fully believe we are all created with a desire for community and connection. My community is one of the biggest blessings in my life. When my life fell apart, the only place I felt safe was with a small group of about three people I talked to on a regular basis. I went from being surrounded by thousands of people as a church leader to being isolated and having communication with only a handful of people.

Often during a traumatic season of life, we choose to isolate out of fear, shame, embarrassment, betrayal, and even exhaustion. Our souls are bruised, and having conversations about our pain is often draining. However, God didn't create us to walk through life alone.

For me, leaning in to my community took work. It took vulnerability, and in some cases, it took repair. It's difficult to lean on community during heartbreak, to trust anyone when your heart literally feels like it is crushed from broken trust. A life of connection and community is risky; however, a life lived in isolation is an even greater risk.

There are people in your life who will hold your story and people who will hear your story. The people who hold your story are the ones who walk with you through the darkest days. They possibly feel some level of the betrayal or pain from the circumstances you're experiencing. One of the differences in holding your story is it's a part of their story. It doesn't mean that anyone knows more of what you experienced, but they possibly carry it more. Your story potentially comes in when they are discussing tough moments in their lives.

I remember when my best friend's husband, Jud, described what Lori experienced when she'd hang up the phone with me. Keep in mind we live two thousand miles apart, and she would call every day. She would say she knew how I was doing based on hearing my voice. Jud said she'd hang up the phone with me and walk straight to his office, lay her head in his lap, and just sob. Her heart broke for me because she was holding my story. My story became part of her story.

Those who hear our story love us and value hearing the vulnerability we're willing to share. Those who hold our story actually felt the weight of our brokenness, were the first people to lock eyes with us after a life-changing event, and carry it differently.

Maybe you are that support system for the person walking through divorce. Here are a few thoughts. We often ask the hurting person, "What do you need?" or "What can I do for you?" or a few other versions of that inquiry, offering authentic help. Here's the catch. A person in trauma doesn't know what they need. So when asked, "What do you need?" they don't know. They don't have an answer. They can't articulate what they need. And honestly, what they do need, you probably can't give them.

Give them options. For instance, you can give specific offers like, "What do you need today? I can come to your house and cook dinner. We can go out for dinner. Or you can come to our house and I'll cook."

Options allow the person in trauma the ability to make a decision and not feel overwhelmed. It helps them to articulate what they need at that time. It helps ground them to feel like they have some control over what is going on around them. When offering help, it's a minor tweak that makes a huge difference.

This played out in my life at sporting events. Showing up alone to events for your kids can be really difficult. You're self-conscious, you're alone, trying to figure out where to sit, who to sit with, and all the while wanting to keep a smile on your face for your kids when your heart is broken.

I went from sitting with multiple family members to being alone. It's hard.

Then this group of five ladies drifted into my life. Our kids had played football together since sixth grade. We'd all been acquaintances since 2014, but something about the football season of 2017 glued us together. They saw I was hurting, and they stepped in. I'm not even sure how we all connected, but they became a lifeline for me in so many ways.

Each game day I'd get a text from one of them or sometimes several of them. The text gave me options. For instance, "Want to meet at the tailgate or want to meet in the stands?" If it was an away game, it would sound more like, "Want us to pick you up, or do you want to meet us at the tailgate?" I didn't even realize at the time how beneficial the options were in allowing me to choose what I was most comfortable with.

I never would have asked for help navigating Friday nights; it just wouldn't have been my nature. They just stepped in and created community every Friday night. Trust me when I say, Friday night games are just one of the many ways these five lovely ladies have shown up for me over the last seven years.

We're now "The Six Pack" because there are six of us, not because of our killer abdominal game—there are way too many kids between us for that. Our kids have long graduated, and we still get together on a regular basis. We share prayer requests, concerns, and gratitudes. We have a group text that contains some of the world's best memes. We have camped together, attended funerals together, celebrated together, and spent loads of time laughing together at happy hour. We always make sure we have a Six Pack Christmas party. There's a beautiful friendship among us that, in some ways, was born out of my need for connection on Friday nights. I would have been lost without them.

Then there are the friendships that feel like they have always existed. The weekend before mediation for my divorce, I flew to meet two of my best friends, Lori Wilhite and Lisa Hughes, and their husbands. These are the two friends who dropped everything and surprised me by flying to Nashville and spending a few nights and days with me on what would have been my twentieth wedding anniversary.

These are the two friends who, over a ten-hour uninterrupted period and lots of Diet Coke, listened to me recount my twenty years of marriage and all the times I felt trust had been shattered, beginning in year one and working chronologically through the relationship. These are the type of friends who, when I gave permission for them to "talk behind my back" (because I grew tired of repeating the details of daily life), responded with, "We already do." And there was never a concern that they were gossiping about me. I knew any conversation they were having "behind my back" was out of genuine concern and love.

Flying to Florida for the weekend, I knew that my heart and my head needed the encouragement, positive feedback, and validation from healthy men who stood on stages and shared the hope of God. Trust me, it isn't lost on me that God placed two friends in my life who are married to pastors, men who held very similar positions to my ex-husband. And clearly, I have no problem being a fifth wheel. Their invitation to fly me to Fort Lauderdale to spend time together for a few days was just what I needed. Their willingness to be with me before the one big day that signified the end of the last twenty years—that's friendship.

During that visit, I had a moment that represented community to me more than just about anything else could. We were at church on Sunday morning and had popped backstage to say hello to an acquaintance of theirs, a woman I had never met but had heard of. Our stories eerily matched, and I could relate to everything she had experienced. The six of us ended up standing in a circle where she and I were directly across from one another, aligned as if looking in a mirror. The reflection I saw was of a woman broken, hurt, defeated, doubting her faith, and ultimately hopeless. She was emotional as she shared a story of what had occurred in her family the night before. As tears streamed down her face, I fought to hold back mine.

The image that came to mind was the story from Exodus 17. Joshua had led the Israelites into battle against the Amalekites, just as Moses had ordered. While Joshua was on the ground fighting, Moses, along with Aaron and Hur, climbed on top of a nearby mountain. While Joshua led the charge on the ground, Moses lifted his hands in prayer to God. While Moses's hands were raised, the Israelites were winning. If his arms lowered out of fatigue, the Amalekites prevailed. The combat lasted for hours, and this is where the story gets good.

So Joshua did what Moses had commanded and fought the army of Amalek. Meanwhile, Moses, Aaron, and Hur climbed to the top of a nearby hill. As long as Moses held up the staff in his hand, the Israelites had the advantage. But whenever he dropped his hand, the Amalekites gained the advantage. Moses' arms soon became so tired he could no longer hold them up. So Aaron and Hur found a stone for him to sit on. Then they stood on each side of Moses, holding up his hands. So his hands held steady until sunset. As a result, Joshua overwhelmed the army of Amalek in battle.

Exodus 17:10–13

Moses could only continue his intercession because of his support system. Aaron and Hur literally held up his arms so he could continue fighting the battle in prayer. We are left with no other option than to believe that if Aaron and Hur hadn't stepped in so Moses could continue to fight the battle with prayer, the Israelites would have been defeated by the Amalekites.

And don't overlook what jumps out in this story. God is the provider of victory when we are attacked. Our attackers might not be armor-wearing, sword-wielding soldiers. The battles may be with familiar faces and well-aimed verbal blows. God is the provider of victory.

God is also the provider of friends to literally hold up our arms when we can't anymore. As women, we are often in the arm-holding business. We support and hold up arms all around us, from our children to coworkers to church friends to neighbors.

This passage in Exodus invites these questions: Who is holding up your arms? Who is joining you in your pain, struggle, hurt, and weariness? Who is grabbing hold of your exhausted hands and helping to lift them to the Lord?

You might be asking how to find these people in your life. Let me share a few characteristics that point to a safe friendship. And if you don't have a friend like this, ask God to bring you the friendship you need.

1. They help you become a better version of yourself.
2. They nurture your talents and abilities.
3. They help connect you with other safe people.
4. They help you develop your spiritual growth.
5. They celebrate your accomplishments and cheer for you.
6. You can put your guard down with them.
7. Vulnerability is welcomed between you.

During my divorce, I specifically remember Lori asking me on a regular basis, "How's your relationship with God?" She didn't just care how I was doing that day, she wanted to make sure I was staying closely connected to the ultimate source of healing, comfort, and peace. People who are concerned about your emotional, physical, and spiritual health are people who can lift your arms. They love you as a whole person and want to support you as you heal and grow. They naturally lift your arms to the point that sometimes you don't even know they're there, until you glance to your right or left and see them next to you.

That passage provides such a promising example for how we should do community with one another: lifting one another's burdens when life throws us something unexpected and heartbreaking. We need friends who cry tears of pain and tears of joy with us.

Backstage after that church service, the value of community in my life made my knees weak and filled my eyes with tears. The four people to my right and my left had lifted my head and helped me dream of better days. They had assured me that even though so much had been lost, God would still use me. The role I filled in the church might be gone, but no one could take God's calling on my life.

Chapter 17 of Exodus ends with praise, and that is the mark of true friendship. Standing across from the lady in Fort Lauderdale was bittersweet. I knew her devastation and heartache, but I also knew a support and love of friends she wasn't experiencing. To my right and left were my modern-day versions of Aaron and Hur, and my heart swelled with gratitude.

When our lives fall apart, we are tempted to hide until we have it all together (or at least the appearance of it). We do ourselves a disservice when we cut ourselves off from others. Often hearing someone say, "Oh, me too, girl," brings more healing than we could ever muster on our own.

Moses knows it's God's power and man's effort working together. Joshua fought, Moses prayed, and God gave the victory. In response to the hard-fought victory, Moses builds an altar—an altar that he calls, "The Lord is my banner" (Exodus 17:15). The Israelites join in praise. Yep, praise—that is the mark of true friendship.

I can't let a chapter on support systems end without mentioning what will eventually become your role down the road in supporting someone else in their suffering. The phrase *give purpose to your pain* is thrown around a lot. In the midst of pain, you don't want it to have purpose as much as you want it to end.

My personal challenge became this: let my suffering become a survival guide for others. The first step in creating that survival guide, and giving purpose to your pain, is to share your suffering. Sharing your suffering isn't always natural or easy. Sometimes it spirals us to the past and can cause what feels like a setback. Only you know when you're ready to share your suffering. You'll know when you've reached a point of healing in order to be able to share. Your story is powerful and needs to be heard by someone who's hurting. Sharing your story brings healing. *Psychology Today* describes the benefits to your body of telling your story.

> Every time you tell your story and someone else who cares bears witness to it, you turn off the body's stress responses, flipping off toxic stress hormones like cortisol and epinephrine and flipping on relaxation responses that release healing hormones like oxytocin, dopamine, nitric oxide, and endorphins. Not only does this turn on the body's innate self-repair mechanisms and function as preventative medicine—or treatment if you're sick. It also relaxes your nervous system and helps heal your mind of depression, anxiety, fear, anger, and feelings of disconnection.[1]

Suffering is where failure and fading of our own desires grows our faith in God. Learning to share my suffering brought freedom I didn't expect. It's become a powerful part of my healing. In my suffering, God taught me how to trust Him, take care of myself, prioritize life, and have healthy relationships. My suffering is what pushed me to complete training to become a life coach and launch a part of my career I could never have dreamed (it's what I like to call my single-mom side hustle).

My suffering has spurred me into this current season of life where I am passionate about helping others get unstuck when life seems hopeless. I have the desire to help guide women walking through transitions that have turned their lives upside down. My suffering helped me realize the importance of continuing to grow my giftings and use my experience to help others process their grief in a way that guides them forward at their own speed.

Suffering helps us realize our strength.

Suffering spurs us on to true healing in Christ.

Suffering teaches us patience with others as they walk their
journey.

Suffering provides us hope that we can share.

Suffering develops our resilience as we walk through other
hard seasons.

Sharing my suffering has connected me with so many single
moms. In fact, during the pandemic I regularly met with this lovely
and incredible small group of single moms on Zoom every two
weeks. A lot of them were in ministry, and they were from all over
the U.S. This group was created out of our shared suffering.

What started as an outlet for single moms who were quarantined
with their kids and might just need an outlet to talk to another adult
became a lifeline. We connected over shared struggles, laughed
over similar single-mom follies, and connected over authentic
concerns. We walked through a book about forgiveness together.
I learned so much from these fellow single moms, like the things
you don't learn in a divorce class.

For instance, I've never known what to call ex-in-laws. I'm still
close to them, I engage with them quite a bit, and I never quite
knew how to introduce them or how to refer to them when telling
a story. Do I say, "my ex's parents," "my kids' grandparents," "my
ex-in-laws"? I was lost; I stumbled through it every time. This group
clarified your ex-in-laws become OUTlaws. Isn't that the best? And
every time I use that phrase, those ladies cross my mind.

Moving toward better than okay takes love, encouragement, and
the lifting of your arms from a valued support system. Living a life
that is better than okay means also being that support system to
others who are suffering.

13

Discarded

How to Find Your Place
When You Feel Like You Don't Fit

I t's a word I hear quite often when talking to women whose marriage has ended. We feel discarded. Discarded by our husband, discarded by friend groups, discarded by the in-laws, discarded from social events, and possibly even discarded by the church. My guess is it's probably a word you've felt at times as well. A label you've experienced that leaves a bad taste in your mouth. It's painful. It hurts.

Part of feeling discarded is realizing you don't know where you fit anymore. Do you still hang out with married couples now that you're single? Possibly you were part of a couple for so long that focusing your attention on just being with singles feels strange.

One thing that I think is often overlooked is that this isn't what we thought our lives would look like. We didn't see this coming or plan for this, so we're doing the best we can, and trying to fit anywhere seems exhausting when you're just trying to survive.

Recently I polled some divorced friends and asked them what things were said to them that left them feeling discarded. Phrases people used that made them feel damaged or abandoned. I was shocked with the honesty of their answers.

"Abusive? Where did he hit you?"

"Get over it and move on."

"Divorce happens every day."

"The kids will be okay."

"You'll be happy when you find someone else."

"Just take him to court."

"You'll be better off."

"If you prayed hard enough, God would answer your prayer
    and bring him back."

"God doesn't like divorce."

"What part did you play in causing him to cheat?"

"When was the last time y'all had sex?"

"We are standing with him."

"You talk a lot; that probably wore him out."

"You're too smart. A man doesn't want to feel like he's in com-
    petition with you."

"He's jealous of you."

"His next wife will have the same experience."

"Were you controlling or needy?"

"Did you put the kids above him?"

"He was abusive? You never had any marks on you."

"He wouldn't do that; he's a church elder."

"God can't use a divorced woman."

"If you were better sexually, he wouldn't need to look somewhere else."

"Maybe you should watch porn with him."

"You should stay, whatever it takes."

Tears spring to my eyes every time I read the above list. The harshness and cruelty is devastating. No wonder so many divorced women feel discarded. Those responses show that we often aren't heard, and if we are heard, we aren't believed, or we're told to just put up with it and move on in the unhealthy situation. My heart breaks for some of the things women have been told about their divorce and how they are identified because of divorce.

There's a cry of injustice that comes with being discarded. Discarded isn't something we asked for or often did anything to cause.

There's a story in the Bible about a servant girl named Hagar who ends up in a situation that I'm sure made her feel discarded. We're told in Genesis 16 that Sarai became impatient with God's timing for the future promised to her and her husband, Abram, so she took matters into her own hands. See, God had told Abram he would be the father of many nations, that his descendants would outnumber the stars in the sky. As the years went by and Sarai grew older and still hadn't become pregnant, she decided she would orchestrate God's promise on her own.

Sarai told Abram to take her Egyptian servant girl, Hagar, as his wife and have a child with her. Hagar quickly became pregnant, and Sarai became jealous. She could no longer stand Hagar and mistreated her. Sarai mistreated Hagar to the point that Hagar finally ran away.

The angel of the LORD found Hagar beside a spring of water in the wilderness, along the road to Shur. The angel said to her, "Hagar, Sarai's servant, where have you come from, and where are you going?" "I'm running away from my mistress, Sarai," she replied. The angel of the LORD said to her, "Return to your mistress, and submit to her authority." . . . Thereafter, Hagar used another name to refer to the LORD, who had spoken to her. She said, "You are the God who sees me." She also said, "Have I truly seen the One who sees me?"

Genesis 16:7–9, 13

The God who sees me. It's so beautiful that during Hagar's discarded season she had an encounter with God, and she describes Him as "the God who sees me."

One thing that's important to note is that when God visits this way, it was the angel of the Lord. This was the first time the angel of the Lord visited anyone. He would later appear to Abraham, Moses, Balaam, Gideon, to name a few. This is the first time the angel of the Lord appeared—to a person who was discarded. He appeared to a single mother-to-be who had been mistreated and ran away.

The other part of this story I love is that Hagar's heart is also changed. Sarai's mistreatment of Hagar partially began because Hagar felt her pregnancy with Abram elevated her above Sarai. Hagar was walking around, pregnant, with an air of supremacy over Sarai. She began to treat Sarai with contempt. When Hagar knew God saw her, she not only went back to Sarai, she submitted to Sarai. Hagar realized it wasn't just her circumstances that needed to change but that she needed to transform as well.

There are times where we write our own personal narrative about being discarded. Sometimes those narratives are justified. And sometimes we allow our hurt to write a story of fiction about being discarded. Always be willing to ask God for truth in the relationship. To show you reality rather than allowing you to create a narrative where you're always the victim.

The feeling of being discarded isn't something that quickly dissipates. Sometimes it lingers when the initial stress and drama of the situation passes. It isn't just during the divorce. It's twelve months later, when life has moved on and people have forgotten that there are times you're still alone. Holidays when your house is empty and you just want someone to see you.

One of the kindest acts I experienced was actually my third Christmas divorced. My kids were gone on Christmas morning. I'd known it was going to happen since the Christmas before. That's how our brains work, right? We work hard to be present for the current holiday we're celebrating because we know next year we won't have our kids for that same celebration.

I'm well loved and had a couple of offers to be with friends, but at the same time, Christmas morning has always been a family time in my mind. There's one set of friends, Stephen and Jackie Brewster, who are extended family, "lifers," as we like to call it, meaning the friendship is for the long haul and we choose to experience life together. They're the family I'd feel totally comfortable spending Christmas morning with, but that year they were out of state visiting family. Jackie and I did a pre-Christmas celebration breakfast on the twenty-third, and when I pulled back into her driveway to drop her off, she told me to wait. She had something she needed to grab for me.

I was in shock when she reappeared at her front door. She and her entire family of six had all shopped for Christmas gifts for me. They were carrying ten wrapped gifts that had been picked out and purchased with loving care. Jackie was raised by a single mom and had a front-row seat to seeing her mom have holidays alone.

Even though they couldn't be in town, they wanted to be able to "celebrate" Christmas morning with me.

That Christmas morning I woke up to an empty house. I was alone (except for my trusty bird dog, who had a stocking full of treats), but I felt seen. With the lights twinkling on the tree and a fire in my fireplace, I slowly unwrapped each gift. Seeing what each member of their family had picked out made me smile and the thoughtfulness of their gifts brought me to tears. I was known. I hadn't been discarded. The gifts reminded me they knew me, they saw me as an extension of their family, and they loved me enough to help me celebrate my Christmas alone. I was cherished and loved.

I'd be remiss if I didn't spend just a tiny bit of time talking about feeling discarded by the church. First, I want to say I'm sorry you might not feel like you fit at church. As a former church leader, I can honestly say you are wanted by churches and church leaders. Sometimes they just don't know how to acknowledge what you've been through. What might feel like being ignored is actually just that they haven't had the experience to know how to best connect with you.

In the following chapter I share a little more about my personal journey in church. I did eventually stop attending and left Cross Point Church, the church I had planted with my then-husband. I'm now attending a microchurch that has been the perfect spot for my family and me in this season.

During a recent Easter service, my pastor used the word *divorce* in his message. As someone who does a little teaching myself, I know one way to draw in the congregation is to list a bunch of scenarios that relate to listeners, something to the effect of:

You received an unexpected medical diagnosis.

You were passed over for a promotion.

Your kid has strayed from God.

Your home is close to foreclosure.

I realized that, within those lists, in regard to marriage relationships, the statement is often something broad and along the lines of, "Your marriage is struggling, your relationship feels like it's ending, you've faced betrayal."

But that day my pastor said, "You received your final divorce decree in your inbox."

My heart skipped a beat when I heard it. Our church is small, and out of the one hundred people in attendance, only two of us are divorced (coincidentally both from pastors, or maybe not so coincidental after all), and still he used the word *divorce* as a scenario.

I felt seen. I felt known. I didn't feel shame.

Divorce hadn't been tiptoed around; it had been stated directly. I've sat through hundreds of messages from lots of gifted communicators in the church, and the term *divorce* is rarely directly stated.

I get it, the response for far too long has been, "God hates divorce." Yep, He does. He hates to see His children hurt. He hates to see the covenant He created broken. He hates to see disloyalty and disrespect between husband and wife.

However, with the divorce rate still high in our society, let's make the church a place where divorced people feel welcomed. We're already self-conscious walking into church alone and feel like all we see is happy families. Create an environment where failed marriages and divorce are discussed and people are not just directed to divorce small groups. Acknowledge single parents, discuss blended families, share in their struggles, and join them in the celebrations.

I think it's not discussed because if you haven't been through it, you don't know. Honestly, I think it's left out because leaders don't know how to recognize divorce in a healthy way; they don't know what divorced people need to hear.

Being divorced doesn't make you second-class. It doesn't mean that God isn't going to use you or allow you to lead. There are lots of men and women who fought hard for their marriage, yet their spouse left. Divorce wasn't an option for them, until it became the only option.

This next section is going to speak to a much smaller section of ladies, but I'd love to just acknowledge the women who were married to pastors and became discarded when their husbands' terrible choices forced an end to their role in church. These women often tirelessly served their churches for many years and, because of their husband's title and his poor decisions, their divorces were thrust into the spotlight.

I'd love to say this is a rare situation and that it usually ends with the church extending a loving and supportive response with actions that show appreciation for the sacrifices that have been made over the years of service, as well as respecting the grief the pastor's wife is experiencing . . . but it doesn't. This is a conversation I've had numerous times. The pastor resigns or is fired, and the entire family unit is dismissed. And that doesn't just mean the discarded wife; it means the innocent children whose lives are in upheaval.

It's where I feel the most frustration: how the hearts of the children, teenagers, and young adults are impacted when they are discarded along with their mothers. The embarrassment and heartbreak they feel is overwhelming when the church their family loved and served discards them. Not only will it affect how they relate to the church in their adult years but, because they are children, it greatly impacts how they will view and interact in their own personal relationship with God.

And this is where I'll say, if the tables were turned and the wife had walked away from the marriage, the husband likely wouldn't be discarded. In fact, in most instances, he'd be celebrated as being a good man who's "doing it all" on his own. He'd keep his job, his friends would still be standing by his side, the board/elder/leadership structure would publicly stand by and support him. And yet the wives and children are so often discarded.

The phone calls I've had with discarded pastors' wives remind me how lucky I was that Cross Point Church continued to walk with me in several ways during and after my divorce. Let me be the first to say I know there isn't a handbook of how to walk through the divorce of a couple in church leadership. I'm aware a lot of people right now will mentally point to *the Bible* . . . and to that I say DUH! That's the ultimate handbook. It's *my* personal, ultimate handbook as well. But there aren't step-by-step instructions, and every situation is different, therefore navigation is difficult.

In fact, I'm going to pause right here and tell you a few of the ways Cross Point loved me as the woman who used to be their pastor's wife.

- They made sure the severance package included the cost of counseling (with the counselor of my choice) for a specified amount of time.
- A group of men showed up and helped demo the house I had purchased to alleviate the cost of construction.
- The staff showed up the morning the boys and I were moving to our new home, packed our U-Haul, drove our U-Haul across town, and unpacked said U-Haul in a matter of about two hours. They were efficient, caring, and full of love. We were feeling a lot of emotions. They met us with smiles and familiar faces and reminded us we weren't alone.

- The creative team purchased and installed the exact same basketball hoop at our new home that my boys had at our old home.
- The small group I had been a part of starting while I was married invited me back into their group.
- People sent an abundance of text messages expressing appreciation and prayers.
- Friends met up for coffee dates to check on my heart and make sure I was doing okay.

Those of you who have been discarded by the church because your pastor-husband made terrible choices, I'm so sorry. My heart breaks for you and your children. I see you and I know how your life has been greatly impacted. I pray God holds you and your kids close and you feel His presence and invite Him into your journey of healing.

Leaders are people too; that I know very well. As leaders we must be aware of how our sin and shortcomings create repercussions in so many people's lives. We're all familiar with the phrase "Hurt people hurt people," and it's true. Let me add an addition to that phrase for you: "Hurt people hurt people. . . . Hurt leaders hurt a lot of people."

Let me share an example that represented to me how layers of hurt can spread out from the actions of leaders. I'm a constant piddler around my house, meaning I'm always moving things around, from room to room or wall to wall. Furniture, plants, art, candles; nothing is safe when my piddling mood strikes. Recently I was moving around some things on my vanity in my bathroom, and I placed my empty glass container for Q-tips on the edge. When I turned around a little too quickly, I knocked that glass container onto my tile floor.

Shards of glass flew. I froze right there in the middle of the broken glass (it never fails, when you break glass you're always barefoot—am I right?). Standing there, I noticed the biggest shards of glass were right where the container had hit the tile, at the point of impact, and the pieces got smaller and smaller the farther out I looked. When I finally moved and began to clean, I found tiny shards of glass eight to nine feet away. How do those small pieces travel that far? Days and even weeks after cleaning up, I was still finding those small remnants of glass tucked away in crevices of the hardwood and hiding in the carpet. A break like that takes an immeasurable amount of cleanup.

When we don't deal with our hurt, when we don't work toward healing our mistakes as leaders, we send shards of hurt, disappointment, and pain through layers and layers of people. The people closest to that leader get hurt the most (the spouse, kids, best friends, the right hand at work), but the hurt ripples far and wide through more people than we often even realize. The pain causes impact for an immeasurable amount of time. The ripple effect of your actions lives far beyond you, so please take the time to deal with the hurt, bravely acknowledge the pain, and find ways to connect.

Please hear me when I say I'm sorry you've felt discarded. Feeling like you don't fit can cause anxiety, self-doubt, and loneliness. You're not alone; we've all felt discarded in some area of our life when navigating divorce. But I encourage you to keep showing up at church, in your small group, at the neighborhood pool, or a community mom's group. You're going to find your fit—it just might take some time.

Be willing to share how you feel. It's going to feel scary to be vulnerable and share that you feel like you don't fit, but people who care about you will meet you in your vulnerability. I remember telling a neighbor how I couldn't find my place when I moved into our new neighborhood. It felt scary admitting I was lost, but her response was so interesting. She acknowledged she had just assumed I knew I was not only accepted but also wanted. She assumed I had enough friends and didn't need her to reach out. In reflection, I realized that if I had reached out to share that I desired connection, she would have met me in my need.

You're going to find your fit. Be patient, keep showing up, and be brave and vulnerable. You'll find the place where you're accepted and wanted.

Stop Trying to Resuscitate What's Dead

How to Breathe Life into Your New Life

"Are we cooperating with the new life waiting to be lived in us, or are we trying to resuscitate the old life because it is all we know?"
—Emily P. Freeman, "123: Practice Your Life"

Isn't it crazy how a quote like the one above happens to pop into your Instagram in the exact season you need it? This quote was a perspective shift for me. An intentional choice to cooperate instead of trying to resuscitate.

My divorce not only signified the end of my marriage, it also produced the end of my role as pastor's wife of a church I loved. God was gracious to heal my heart pretty quickly in regard to the loss of my ex-husband: I have never missed him in my life. I've gotten lonely, I've grieved the loss of the family I dreamed of. But I've never missed him as an individual.

But man did I miss Cross Point.

Not necessarily my role as much as the intentional community, the loving staff family, and being part of something God-ordained. Sundays and Tuesdays (which were all-staff meeting days) hit hard for a few years. I would still pop in occasionally for Sunday services to see staff and enjoy worship, but at the same time, I knew Cross Point wasn't going to be my church home any longer. Too much had occurred, the loss was immense, and moving on was the best decision for me and my family.

Where I live in the South hosts an abundance of churches; surely finding a new church home would be easy. I visited so many churches. Big churches, small churches, churches that were different stylistically, churches that had different methodology, worship styles, and meeting spaces. I was trying, I really was. But my heart was trying to resuscitate what I'd lost, my old life.

A perspective shift was needed.

Finding a church home was on my prayer list for years. Regularly I asked God to find us a church that felt safe and provided the intentional community we longed for. At a casual, every-six-month-ish catch-up lunch with a neighbor, I asked about visiting the church where her husband was on staff, when the conversation took a sharp turn and she shared they were going to start a church in their home. That simple statement stirred up such emotion for me, my eyes filled with tears. Immediately I told her I was interested and asked if I could be added to their small list of potential families. My emotion was still so strong when I got back in my car after lunch that I recorded a voice memo on my phone to remember how I knew God was stirring my heart. The lunch transitioned from being a time to catch up and chat to clearly being God-ordained in my heart. The emotion stirring inside of me felt like God reminding me He knew what I needed and was going to continue to provide.

A few weeks later I attended their first informational meeting for a microchurch model that meets in homes. To be honest, it felt strange at first; it wasn't what was familiar to me. Cross Point was one of the fastest-growing churches in the nation, the largest church in Middle Tennessee . . . and here I was attending a home church with thirty people. I was a megachurch church girl in a microchurch world. And I felt comfortable. And safe. And wanted. And accepted. Talk about a change in perspective.

Fast forward a few months to a snowy Sunday in Tennessee, and we had our first official church meeting together. The roads were icy, snow was still falling, but my new church was less than one mile down the street.

That first Sunday morning, I took a deep breath and walked into a house full of people who were also seeking an intentional community with other believers. Community within a church was something that had been absent from my life for almost five years, yet my heart longed for that kind of community on a daily basis. My soul slowly began to entertain the thought of engaging with a new spiritual community and beginning to build new relationships in the structure of a church body.

I was slowly cooperating with the new life God had for me, but it was a process, and when it comes to our personal growth, we have to trust the process. Trusting the process wasn't always easy. I'll let you in on a little personal private processing of that growth; for the first year of attending the home church, I never parked in the driveway. I always parked on the side street facing the exit onto the main road. Parking in the driveway felt like I could get trapped and not get out when I wanted. Remember, this was a safe environment, yet I always needed to know I could exit whenever I wanted. My hyperfocus on possibly needing to escape from church was a real issue. A large part of me wondered if I could really do church community again, or was I too damaged? Could the people of the house church be trusted? Was I opening myself up to being hurt once again? Those triggers were real, and I was finally ready to deal with them. It was time for me to lean into the triggers I was experiencing in order to heal and rewrite my story in regards to the church.

Fast forward about ten months, and in mid-December we experienced a terrible thunderstorm. Living in the South, we usually spend a couple nights a year hunkered in an inner-room bathtub for protection from possible tornadoes. This night was one of those nights. The storm ravaged through our neighborhood, and after repeated lightning strikes, I knew we had some damage to large trees in our backyard.

As the sun rose the next morning, I opened the back door to survey the damage. We'd lost one massive ash tree and about half of a really large oak tree. The limbs grazed the three steps leading up to my home. Basically, we were about twelve to eighteen inches shy of having a tree come through the roof and into our family room.

I'm a pretty independent person. I've managed home remodels, done plenty of DIYs, and handled some minor electrical and plumbing tasks. But uproot a couple of trees in my backyard, and I'm lost. Unfortunately I don't own a chainsaw, nor do I know how to correctly use one.

To be honest, I stood at a very distinct crossroad. I knew I could call some men from Cross Point to come and take care of the trees and they would show up, love me well, and handle the situation.

For me at that stage, that would have been trying to resuscitate my old life, what I had lost.

God was calling me to cooperate with the new life He was offering.

To be honest, I wanted both. I was straddling between two churches. I wanted to resuscitate my old and also cooperate with the new. But that isn't full healing. That isn't trust. Faith isn't present in the straddling. True connection couldn't happen in the old or in the new if I continued to straddle.

Through a series of texts and phone calls, within a few hours, some men from my new church showed up with chainsaws and went to work. That decision symbolically represented the passing of the baton of my heart from my old life into my new life and church family.

Letting go of Cross Point had been terribly hard. I loved that church deeply. What I know to be true about myself is that I love deeply, so I hurt deeply . . . AND I also heal deeply.

Upon reflection in my journal, I identified two significant components in the cooperation of my heart.

1. It took time. I had to wait.
2. God was at work through it all.

Because I knew that probably wouldn't be the last time I'd experience straddling between old and new, I made a timeline in order to *see* how God had been working out my fervent prayer for a new church family.

God's timeline for me and the house church

November 2020—Lunch with Audrey when she tells me they are starting a church

February 2021—Sticking my toes in the water of the house church

March to October 2021—Slowly digging in, showing up, and becoming vulnerable in sharing

November 2021—Pastor Chris asked me to be part of Lead Team

December 2021—Tree down in our yard and making the decision to lean in to the new house church rather than the familiar (Cross Point)

January 2022—Visited early service at Cross Point to celebrate a friend's baptism. It was beautiful to be there. Afterward, I got in my car and wasn't angry about what was taken from me; I was grateful. Grateful to go "home" to my regular service at the house church.

This simple timeline helps me remember God is always at work to accomplish His plan for our lives. It also represents what waiting can look like and how the puzzle pieces of our life fall into place to craft His vision for our futures. And most importantly, just because I can't see His plan doesn't mean there isn't one. In future seasons of waiting, I'll now have this reminder of His goodness.

I believe God's timing is best. But waiting for life to unfold in His timing can be tough at times. Second Corinthians 4:8 tells us, "We are pressed on every side by troubles, but we are not crushed. We are perplexed, but not driven to despair."

What does that look like when you're walking the journey of divorce? You are pressed on every side by troubles. I know I was. But I wasn't crushed. I was damaged, but not destroyed. How do we feel pressed but not crushed? How do we walk through times when we are perplexed and not be driven to despair?

What I have learned about life is *my focus matters*! I recently turned forty-eight, and I feel pretty good about that, but there's one area that makes me officially feel middle-aged. My readers.

Yep, I have around seven pairs, including a pair of sunglasses for the pool. They can be found in the kitchen, hanging on the front of my shirt, in the bedroom, on the desk in my office, on my head, and in my clutch. You might think I have a problem. I'm betting you just haven't hit forty-three yet. But I can't focus and read the small print without them. I've even left old lady comments on my younger friends' Instastories saying, "Your older and wiser friend can't read that microscopic font."

What do these glasses have to do with our current troubles, our failed marriage, our heartache? They remind us where to focus.

Focus your point of view. Point of view is a tricky thing. I actually have a master's degree as a reading specialist, so I have taught point of view to third and fourth graders more times than I can count; however, I hadn't applied it to my personal story. In the midst of my troubles, I believed that God could give my pain a purpose, but for a long time, that felt like I had to relive the pain of my divorce over and over. My dear friend Lori would teasingly say, "Brandi has a divorce ministry she never wanted." She was right. Talking about my divorce didn't feel like moving forward. Revisiting that pain wasn't a healthy emotional space for me.

For me to be able to use my pain for purpose, I had to shift my point of view.

A different set of lenses

One way to think about this played out is on one of my favorite television shows, *This Is Us*. In season 2, Randall has a quote I just love. It's after a family counseling session (mom and three siblings) while Kevin is in rehab for alcohol abuse, and a huge disagreement breaks out. Lots of "That isn't how it happened" and "I never did that," and it turns into utter chaos with everyone objecting and talking over one another. Later, after the siblings come together again, Randall says, "I think everyone sees their childhood with different lenses, different perspectives."[1]

The story of our life is the same; we need to see it through a new set of lenses. For me, my story moves from being about divorce to focusing on single moms. I have had the opportunity to travel and speak a few times to groups of single moms, and that is so life-giving to me: encouraging them, being vulnerable with my pain so they feel validated in theirs, sharing our struggles of supporting our kids, discussing the difficulties that can come with running and managing a single-parent home. I'm sharing the same story, just from a different point of view.

I choose to move from just seeing my divorce to seeing how I can help coach people through transitions in life. Sharing my experience and hearing them share theirs. To use my story to mentor those going through something similar. To talk through the unique challenges of major life transitions . . . facilitate them as they take one day at a time. To have compassion for those who are facing immense hurt from a leader in their life. To be an empathic listener and help solve what they are facing. To remind them, in the midst of disappointment and heartache, that we will be better than okay.

One of the prayers at the top of my list was for opportunities and guidance in my career. I was working the nonprofit job I loved but also felt that I might be able to do something on the side to help supplement my salary, a little single-mom side hustle, if you will. The first time I shared my story post-divorce was in October of 2017 to a group of ministry leaders at our Leading and Loving It event in Vegas—yep, you read that correctly, church leaders in Vegas! As confident as I was about my message, I was still hesitant to be the "divorced megachurch pastor's wife." It wasn't a title I embraced . . . at all.

I'm the first to admit at times I have tunnel vision, and I couldn't see outside my "divorced" bubble. Until my phone rang less than two weeks after I stood on stage, sharing my story for the first time, and a number that wasn't in my contacts appeared. Typically, I would assume it was spam and never answer, but this time I did. A fellow ministry leader from a large church on the other side of town was on the line, and she said something that totally shifted my point of view. Each year in November, their church celebrates single moms with a day of encouragement, gifts, and a reminder that they are not forgotten. But the keynote speaker had canceled for health reasons. She asked me, "I know this is a long shot, with very short notice, but any chance you would come and share your story with these single moms?"

Just like that, I saw my story through a new set of lenses. The focus became my story as a single mom, which felt strong and hopeful. Essentially, it's the same story, but being able to mentally stand in my truth as a single mom brought a new strength and endurance that seeing myself as the divorced pastor's wife couldn't provide.

Since that first single mom's event, I've connected with more single moms than I ever thought possible. As I mentioned in an earlier chapter, during the pandemic, I hosted Zoom rooms for single moms, since a lot of us were quarantined with our kids and needed an adult outlet. I've spoken at various conferences and Mother's Day celebrations for single moms. Through my work at Leading and Loving It, we've been able to bring awareness to single moms around the holidays and provide small gifts of appreciation and encouragement.

None of this would have happened if I hadn't shifted my focus. If I hadn't begun to look at my life through the lens of "single mom" rather than "divorced pastor's wife."

For me to be able to discover the purpose of my pain, I had to shift my point of view. It's the same messy yet beautiful story, where I don't have all the answers, but as I shared the redemption of my heart, I realized that hurting people don't need us to be perfect—they need us to be present. Often we need to see our heartbreak through a new set of lenses. I used my story to encourage other single moms by being vulnerable with my own pain, so that they felt validated in theirs, and by sharing in the struggles of emotionally supporting our kids.

I shared the same stories, just sometimes from a different point of view: a point of view that is life-giving to my heart. My perspective started changing from viewing my *To be continued* . . . season as a daunting threat to a hopeful mantra. Though there is pain in the night, God's mercies are new every morning. Cooperating with the new life God has for you means the pain isn't the end of you; pain is the opportunity for new life, for hope, for healing.

Take some time today and this week to think about where you're focusing. Evaluate the perspective with which you view your pain. How can you shift your focus in order to give purpose to your pain? What are you trying to resuscitate that's dead? Most importantly, where does God want to breathe new life into your story, and are you willing to cooperate with Him in the new life He has for you?

Brandi Got Her Groove Back

How to Navigate the Peaks and Pitfalls of Dating

D*ating.* Be prepared: Plenty of people who are married are going to tell you how fun dating again is. *Fun* isn't a word I'd use to describe dating. It's not terrible, but it takes some work. Also, let's define dating. Being a parent of teenage boys, I learned that terminology in regard to relationships is very important. For instance, the different stages of a relationship as defined by teenagers can be described as talking, a thing, exclusive, and dating. For the purposes of this chapter, *dating* is meeting single men and going on dates. *Dating* is getting back in the game after years of marriage. I'm not talking about a relationship, but rather a casual, get-to-know-you date, in hopes of finding a person you'd like to be in a relationship with.

Let me tell you, there is a unique type of suffering associated with having three teenage boys and braving dating again. In general, dating at my age feels like suffering. Put the two together—dating and having teenage sons—watch out! All my boys handle my dating in different ways.

Brewer, my youngest, introduced me to his friend, inserting the juicy tidbit of information that his friend's dad is divorced. I thought, *Oh, good, he has another friend from a divorced family!* Then, much to my shock, I realized he told me that piece of info to play matchmaker.

Gage, my middle son, went on a rant, adamantly telling me how weird it would be if I went out with one of his friends' dads . . . which I already had, unbeknownst to him. Twice.

Jett, the oldest of my boys, is the hardest one to navigate around, as he's super protective. As a single mom, I have realized that it was easier to be a nineteen-year-old girl coming in from a date to my forty-six-year-old father than it was to be a forty-six-year-old woman coming home from a date to my nineteen-year-old son! One evening a little after eleven, I came home from a dinner date to a dark house. Assuming my kids were all in bed, I tiptoed through the kitchen and toward the family room with only the light of my phone. As I turned the corner into the family room, I was greeted by a male voice stating, "You missed curfew." My immediate response was, "Yes, sir," before I quickly remembered I am the adult, I don't have a curfew. Yes, my nineteen-year-old son waited up for me.

A few quick thoughts you're probably already aware of . . .

Dating has changed a lot since you were a teenager.

Dating is work.

Prepare for more mediocre and bad dates than good dates.

I've found one of the biggest challenges of dating is meeting people. I primarily work from home with my two dogs. They think I'm pretty special, but they're for sure not introducing me to anyone. And I'm lucky to still have a lot of married friends, but their single-friend group basically consists of me. So what's a girl in her forties to do?

Dating apps

Yep, I tried them.

Yep, I have stories (aka The Handsy Italian, The Married Man, and The Gay Dad).

Yep, I would tell other single people to give them a try.

Also, it doesn't escape me that one evening in December a few years back, my oldest son was swiping on a dating app while I was sitting across the room swiping on a different dating app. It's the world we live in.

Don't feel ashamed if you choose to use a dating app. It's almost like people shy away from admitting it unless they make a match and begin an actual relationship. Admitting you're trying an app to meet people tends to come with a bit of embarrassment, and it shouldn't. You're working toward meeting someone, you're getting outside your comfort zone and trying something that might feel scary to you, you're putting yourself out there and finding the confidence to engage with someone of the opposite sex. Why feel embarrassed?

Rejection?

Shame?

Fear of failure?

Possibility of experiencing another heartbreak?

Insecurity?

Not being chosen?

Doubting your value?

All of those are understandable reasons. But I think we've already come to the agreement that we aren't going to allow our past to hold us back. We've done enough of that. We are older and wiser now. We know what we want in life. We know what we won't tolerate. We have experienced some level of unhealthy patterns and dysfunction we don't want to face in a future relationship.

Here are a few lessons I learned about dating apps.

○ Don't give out your number too quickly.

○ Have a male friend you respect read and offer helpful suggestions to your dating profile. I had a married couple in their second marriage with a blended family give really specific feedback on what I wanted in my profile. It was so helpful. He tweaked what I was looking for into terms that men would understand and connect with.

○ Have preset guidelines for dates. For instance, I typically did a happy hour during the week. It gave me an easy out for the date not to go too long because usually I had a commitment following.

○ Be honest. If they ask for a second date and you're not feeling it, kindly tell them. Don't ghost. We're adults. Tell them you wish them the best. I kept a prewritten text that was kind, honest, and direct in the notes app on my phone and would personalize it to each situation. That way I didn't put off responding or stress about what to say.

○ Take breaks. There were times the communication wasn't enjoyable. When I felt that dread coming on, I'd pause my profile and take a break. Sometimes for a few weeks and sometimes for a few months at a time. There were times when it felt like a job, and that's a clear sign you need to take a break.

○ Google is your friend. Use it to make sure who you're meeting is legit. I don't always recommend a deep dive, but it is nice to know the person you're meeting is who they say they are.

○ Try a date or two outside of your typical type. You might be pleasantly surprised. Many of us have a type we're attracted to. Dating outside that type can introduce you to some interesting people.

Since I've been an open book thus far, why stop and get all private with my dating life now? The biggest thing I can probably stress is to know yourself and what you're looking for. I stated above that you should know what you won't tolerate. Be aware of red flags. But also be on the lookout for green flags. We often focus on what to run from; there is also a massive benefit in knowing what we should look for in a relationship.

Examples of green flags

Someone who creates a safe place for you to be vulnerable and is also vulnerable themselves.

Someone who is kind and respectful to others, even strangers you might encounter on dates.

Someone who is able to say "I'm sorry."

Someone who respects your boundaries.

Someone whose words match their actions.

Someone who respects your emotions, words, and beliefs.

Someone who is capable of hard conversations.

Someone who is respectful during conflict and moves toward repair.

Someone who is self-aware and can take ownership when needed.

Someone who prioritizes their personal growth.

Someone who has other healthy relationships with friends and family members.

This isn't an exhaustive green-flag list. But I believe there is value in knowing what to look for and what helps create a secure and safe relationship.

Here are a few other things to consider in regard to dating.

1. Everyone decides to date again at their own pace

Some people are ready to get back out there. Others will take more time to feel comfortable before diving back into the dating pool. This is another area where you're in control. Date when you feel ready. Don't allow others to decide when you're ready to date; you'll know. Trust your intuition on when to date and the people you meet.

I'll be honest, I might have tried dating too soon. There was something about feeling so rejected by my former spouse that made me want to see if I would always be rejected. I know I dated too soon because I rarely used the person's name when telling friends about my date. I referred to them by occupation. For instance, here's a typical conversation I might have with a girlfriend after a date.

Girlfriend—"How was your date with the police officer?"

Me—"It went okay, not sure there was a spark, but he was kind and respectful."

Girlfriend—"Is he the one with three kids?"

Me—"Nope, that is the Realtor."

Girlfriend—"Oh, the police officer doesn't have kids, right?"

Me—"Actually he has four; the accountant doesn't have kids."

It might sound silly, but by not using names, it allowed me to not really connect with dating. It felt more like a life someone else was experiencing, but not something I was willing to connect with yet.

2. Decide what you want out of dating

There were times I dated for practice. That's right. I hadn't dated since I was nineteen, and I was out of practice in carrying on conversation in a dating scenario. I know that doesn't sound romantic or even fun. But the mindset of practice felt like less pressure. It also allowed me to meet some interesting men and engage in conversation on a variety of topics. The practice also was a great boost for my self-esteem. It gave me the courage to show up and get comfortable being me instead of some version of me I thought might be more appealing.

3. Decide what you're looking for

Once I was single, it didn't take long for me to fall into my regular rhythm that kept me focused and start a list. Yep, a list of what I wanted in a future partner. The list was always the last page of the current journal I was using, and I just jotted down important characteristics as they crossed my mind.

I chose to be very specific about details some might deem as un important, for instance: tall, drives a truck, and has a beard. The list also included personality details like loves to laugh, witty, pursuer of me, and a caretaker. I recorded important character traits too: loyal, committed, loves God and has his own relationship with Him, communicates without guilt or manipulation, and values equality in relationship. I didn't walk into dates and use this as a checklist. In fact, I'd go months and months without adding anything to it. But if I met someone who had a quality I hadn't experienced, I'd jot it down on my list. I was aware of my list, but not tied to it. The list clarified what I valued and what was important to me.

4. Give yourself the grace to make mistakes

Even with the clarity I tried to take into dating, I made lots of dating mistakes!

When I first started dating, I took the discussion too deep too quickly. I didn't mean to, but because I was doing so much deep, personal work on myself, that was where I would take discussions with someone who was a virtual stranger. Because I was so aware of relational dysfunction from my past relationship, I sure didn't want to end up in that scenario again, so I dove into chats about therapy, self-awareness, and personal patterns way too quickly.

It was too early to be concerned and focused on their emotional health and intelligence. Time needed to be spent just getting to know them and figuring out if we had anything in common. How did they spend their free time? What hobbies did they enjoy? Which sports teams did they cheer for? What is their favorite type of food? Simple and easy getting-to-know-you information. Emotional health and intelligence were high on my list of desired traits in a future partner, but I didn't need to spend so much time invested in their emotional health on a first date.

Which brings me to my second dating mistake: the filter I created to determine if I wanted to see them again. I knew I wanted to be in a permanent relationship again, but I also didn't feel the need to hurry into marriage. I was content living life single. Yet the filter I used on each first date was "Will I marry him?"

WHATTHEHECK—of course the answer to the question was always going to be an astounding "No!" because you don't know the answer after one date. I was probably two years into my dating journey when my dear friend gently said, "Maybe you'd find more success in dating if you asked yourself, *Do I want to go on a second date with them?* rather than if you want to marry them."

That shifted my perspective. It felt like less pressure and allowed me to relax and enjoy myself a little more. It allowed me to just be present in the moment and not jump into the future. That filter allowed me to lean into getting to know someone and not analyzing them.

Another mistake that, once corrected, created a huge mental shift was moving my focus from "Will they like me?" to "Do I like them?" The "Will they like me?" mentality was exhausting, so I switched to the question that was way more important: "Do I like them?" And that was a game changer.

We often walk into dating needing affirmation or so desiring a positive interaction with the opposite sex that we don't take the time to ask ourselves if we actually like the person. We're too focused on being charming, interesting, and engaging in order to be liked. And often not focused enough on whether we like them. Finally, I got to the point where, before I opened a door to walk in to meet someone, I'd tell myself, "They are so lucky to get to spend the next hour with me!" Believe that about yourself! Believe they are lucky to get to meet someone like you. Whether you have a second date or not, they got the opportunity to meet you.

Be aware that you might be drawn to what your marriage was missing. That isn't necessarily a good thing. For instance, maybe you are very independent, and your ex never called during the workday to check on you. Independent or not, it's nice to know someone is checking in. You go on a couple of dates with the same guy, and he begins to call and check on you during the day. Initially it's once a day and that's nice, but it quickly moves to multiple times a day and you realize he's controlling and too interested in how you spend your time. Initially it seemed nice because it was something your marriage lacked, but that doesn't mean it's healthy. Go slowly—you're in no rush and on no timeline except the one you create and are comfortable with.

5. Seek your own emotional health first

Here's my biggest piece of dating advice: The healthier you are emotionally, the emotionally healthier you attract. An emotionally stronger me creates an emotionally stronger we. It's true. I can't emphasize enough the need to deal with your own baggage before launching into another relationship. Falling in love again doesn't fix your life. Dealing with your emotional history will. You're not the same person you were when you got divorced. Continuing to focus on your own personal emotional health will greatly impact your next relationship. Not only does it allow you to attract healthier partners, it will also allow you to spot unhealthy partners more quickly. And I'm gonna say it one more time; an emotionally stronger me creates an emotionally stronger we.

Speaking of baggage, here's another truth: At this stage of life, we all have baggage. We're at the point in our lives where we all are dealing with disappointment, unmet expectations, grief from a failed marriage, abandonment, and possibly even betrayal. Lighten that baggage before embarking on another journey with a partner. Identify what you need to heal from, and spend time invested in yourself.

I know that probably has become the broken-record message of this book. But if you want to live a life that is better than okay, work on yourself. NOT because you're broken or damaged, but because you want to move forward in a healthy, fulfilling relationship. Because you don't want to repeat past mistakes or unhealthy patterns. What you don't repair, you repeat.

Embarking on the dating journey again was a bit overwhelming. But the thought that bounced around in my head repeatedly was, *Will I ever be able to trust again?* I'd been in a relationship of repeated broken trust. I'd encountered feeling verbal and emotional abuse. Would I ever be able to put past hurts aside, or would I carry those forward?

Will I ever trust anyone again?

That's a question I've asked myself and also been asked numerous times. One evening at a dinner with a few girlfriends, one of them quoted therapist Jim Cress. Jim had explained that trust is time plus believable behavior. Or as I see it in my head . . .

$$TIME + BELIEVABLE\ BEHAVIOR = TRUST$$

The visual made me recognize that both of those components are measurable. Trust is a concept that, up until that point, I believed either happened or didn't happen. With this definition I could look at what more precisely builds trust between two people.

Believable behavior—Do their words match their actions? Do they call when they say they'll call? Do they show up for you? Are they willing to hear you and what matters to you? Do you feel valued and appreciated by them? Believable behavior can match any of the green flags listed above.

Time—A measurable period together.

What's great about this formula is that it allows space for trust to grow. The longer you are with someone, the more opportunity you have to experience their believable behavior. The more believable behavior you see over time, the more trust can be built.

Dating again also brought a fear to the front lines that I hadn't expected. *Do I trust myself to survive the possibility of engaging with someone who could break my heart again? I don't want to ever experience that level of hurt from another individual in my lifetime, and if I did, I'm not sure I'd survive it.* That fear bounced around in my head more than I wanted to admit. The fear of experiencing that level of betrayal and suffering from another individual I loved.

During a conversation with a friend where I vulnerably shared my fear, she shared the wisest illustration that I'd love to pass on to you as you face your fears about dating, moving forward, and learning to trust someone. She compared the emotional and mental healing to a bulletproof vest. She reminded me, "When your husband left, your life was shattered, your heart was broken, and you were lost. But you also made the decision to seek health and growth. You've done a lot of hard work on yourself and how to be the healthiest and most confident version of you. Why don't you think of all of that hard work like a bulletproof vest. Chances are you could get hurt again, but the work you've done means you will be more protected this time around." And she's right, I'm not at all the same person I was seven years ago when my husband left. The work I've done has changed how I engage in relationships and how I show up for myself. It's another reason I encourage you to take care of yourselves, friends. The work you do while single will impact what dating looks like for you and also how you react when disappointment happens.

Oftentimes divorce leaves us not trusting ourselves. Whether it's because we enabled bad behavior or forgave one too many times, we worry about making the same mistakes again.

Because of your growth and work toward healing your heart, you aren't the same person you were then, and when it comes to dating, you're going to need to learn to trust your gut. If something feels off, get curious and ask questions. If it feels like you aren't being told the truth, trust your gut and investigate. The opposite can also be said; if someone feels like they are a really good person, full of kindness and emotionally healthy, trust your gut. You're in no rush in regard to dating. You create your own timeline. Remember, you are in charge of your dating life. You're in control of who you do and don't spend time with.

After more than five years single, I entered an exclusive dating relationship. I did loads of first dates during those five years, but only a handful of second dates. Through a setup by friends, I met someone I've enjoyed getting to know, who I prioritize investing my time in, and with whom I desire to learn how to do life together. I bring it up in this chapter because I wanted to introduce a phrase he and I have learned as a dating couple—*family-first dating*.

As you know, I have three sons, and he has two children of his own. Our kids are all in a similar age range. I have my boys two-thirds of the time, and his parenting plan is fifty-fifty. We both work full-time jobs, and most weeks average over forty hours of work. We both love parenting and consider it our greatest role. I bring up family-first dating because I didn't realize the work it would take to make sure you're keeping your kids a priority as you're falling in love with someone.

Family-first dating is one of those good news–bad news scenarios. It has been healthy because it creates some natural boundaries. When you're falling in love, you want to be with that person as much as possible; when you're parenting five kids between you, that isn't possible. We have practices, games, obligations, orthodontist appointments, and these kids need dinner each night. There's not much space for "drop everything and meet up." The time boundaries are healthy and hard.

We've had to get creative. We have a standing weekly lunch date, just to make sure we have time in person each week. As much as I don't enjoy talking on the phone (thirteen-year-old Brandi would be shocked by that statement), I make time to talk to him each day. Occasionally we invite one another into our time with our kids. Just want to give you a heads-up if you are a parent and enter into a dating relationship: It is going to have different struggles than you experienced when you were dating before. The struggles aren't bad, they are just what life looks like for you currently.

And as difficult as family-first dating is to figure out at times, being with someone who has done their emotional work, is self-reflective, is a great dad, is respectful to and values me, and has a relationship with God has more than been worth figuring out time, balancing each other's family, and connecting and growing together. Don't settle in dating. Hold out for what you want and know you deserve, and try to have some fun along the way.

There's a scene in one of my favorite shows, *Ted Lasso*, where Rebecca, a middle-aged businesswoman, has started dating again. The scene helped remind me what I was looking for in dating. In the episode "Goodbye Earl," Rebecca's been on a double date with her best friend, Keeley, and Keeley's boyfriend, Roy Kent.

I love this scene and the reminder of what we deserve (love this scene, but also removed Roy's overuse of foul language). Roy's overhearing the conversation Keeley and Rebecca are having as they break down characteristics of the man she's been dating. There are lots of boring details, and as the list continues, Roy interrupts the ladies. They both look in his direction, curious. Then Roy gets honest: "Tell the truth. He's fine. That's it. Nothing wrong with that, most people are fine. It's not about him, it's about why . . .

you think he deserves you. You deserve someone who makes you feel like you've been struck by . . . lightning. Don't you dare settle for fine!"[1]

As you date, remember it's not about him. It's about why you think he deserves you, because you deserve someone who makes you feel like you've been struck by lightning. Don't you dare settle for fine!

2,400 Square Feet and a Prayer

How to Start Dreaming Again

In the midst of living a life I loved as a mom, I'd stopped dreaming for myself. Don't get me wrong, I had dreams for my family and dreams for my boys. But I'd stopped dreaming specifically for Brandi.

And I was okay with it, honestly. I probably hadn't even noticed that I didn't dream about what I wanted my future to look like, what I wanted to achieve, where I wanted to go in life. When I thought about my future outside of being a wife and mom, life was pretty blank. That doesn't mean I didn't have a lot going on, but I was living life aimlessly.

After a particularly difficult conversation with a family member, he hugged me and said, "Dream big." At the time I thought how sweet it was of him to view my life that way; what I realized is *I* wasn't viewing my life that way. I had always let others dream for me, and it was time to learn to dream for myself. To dream about my life and what God had in store for me. To dream using the strength and clarity I was experiencing to examine what I really wanted, how I wanted my life to be intentionally lived.

I had to begin to dream again. My guess is the same might be true of you. Your marriage is ending, and part of beginning again is learning to dream for yourself . . . and you're lost. I've been there. I know what a struggle it is to think about dreams for your life.

Yet no one wants to live life without direction. As humans, we crave purpose for our lives. We want to make a difference. Dreaming about your future brings anticipation and excitement. It allows you to see the endless possibilities of your life, not just the life you've lived that's familiar. Familiarity isn't bad, but dreaming is another opportunity for you to put back together the pieces of your life the way you want.

Here's where I admit that while learning to dream for yourself is vitally important, I was lost on how to start. Maybe you're having a similar reaction as you read this. Dreaming again sounds great, but where do you begin? Here are a few suggestions to dream for yourself again.

Begin to dream in small ways

The first area where I began to dream was one that was natural to me: our home. I knew I was going to be selling the home my family had lived in for twelve years for financial reasons, as well as because I wanted a space that was new to us and didn't have any painful memories. There was a lot I didn't know—you're gonna hear more about that pretty soon. But what I did know was how I wanted our home to feel and what I wanted our home to represent. So I did what I always tend to do when I have ideas bouncing around in my head. I made a list.

- Mostly white walls
- Lots of live plants
- My bedroom painted navy blue (side note: the color scheme on this cover is also the color scheme of my house—I'm consistent) ;)
- Lots of soft blankets and comfy pillows
- A relaxing outdoor space
- Firepit in the back
- All white bedding in my room
- A safe place to begin again
- Layers of texture
- Candles I didn't just buy but also burned
- House of TRUTH

The list was super simple, but it helped me begin to dream. Dream about what I valued in my home, as well as the atmosphere and feeling I wanted to create for my family.

It was freeing for so many reasons. Approval for paint colors wasn't needed by anyone else. I didn't ask anyone about furniture choices. I chose what I wanted in our home. I created the budget. I was decisive and empowered. Dreaming and executing was beginning to get easier with that one step.

What's an area of your life that is natural for you? Mine is creating a comfortable and cozy home, so it was easiest to begin in an area where I already felt comfortable. I was dreaming about a home that, when I started the list, didn't yet exist. I didn't have an address or even an inkling of where the boys and I would start over. But I like to create safe and comfortable spaces, and I knew I wanted to give all four of us a fresh start.

What is something that you know is going to happen? Although I knew we would be moving, I had no idea where. But moving was a for-sure thing for the four of us. I chose to start with something I knew was going to be part of our future. The dream was realistic and essential. Sure, dreaming about winning the lottery and never again facing financial hardship is fun, but it wasn't a realistic and essential dream in my life. Dream about what is already going on around you.

Investigate what you've left in your past that's part of who you are at your core

Often, important pieces of ourselves get left behind when our marriage falls apart. Photos from a past life can be hard to see. It's when Timehop can really create some strong emotional responses. I recently shared some photos of the Quarter Horse I owned when I was married with a new friend who knew nothing about my love of horses. Growing up in rural Kentucky, horses were a large part of my childhood, and many memories and hours were spent atop my first pony, Missy. Horses almost seem like second nature to me.

When I was married we owned some acreage about an hour outside of Nashville. That space allowed me to engage again in my love of horses. It wasn't long before a couple of equines resided on our property. The horse trainer I hired for my horse focused on Natural Horsemanship, and learning a new method was challenging in the best way. I felt like I was engaging a different part of my brain and almost rediscovering why horses are such magical creatures. The two-hour training session each week was always special to me. I was focused on doing something just for me.

When the divorce happened, I no longer had access to the farm, nor did I have a place close to home to board the horse. She stayed at the farm my ex-husband kept and she was eventually sold. And I haven't engaged with horses since.

I realized as I shared my love for horses with my new friend that, in moving on from my past, I'd actually left behind some parts of myself I really like. Sometimes it's hard to move on from the past and still embrace the pieces of that life you enjoy. A few things I was reminded about myself:

- I love working with horses.
- I'm definitely country at heart.
- I have no problem getting dirty and living a farm life.

When walking through grief, we often cut off all parts of our past in order to heal. And in learning to walk through life post-divorce, we leave behind some things we love. Take some time to evaluate what you've left behind in your past life that actually is part of who you are.

It's even beneficial to think back to who you were pre-marriage and how you spent your time. Remember who *she* was before she became a *we*.

Bring God into your dreams—He wants you to have the desire of your heart

One of the prayers I repeated in my journal almost daily was for a house for the boys and me to have a fresh start. A lot of people want to keep their home post-divorce. I felt strongly that our old home contained too many memories, and after all the pain we'd walked through, I felt a fresh start was best. Plus I wanted to make a wise financial decision and live in a home that fit my new budget.

So I began to journal about our future home. The boys and I began to talk about moving. One night over dinner we had a family meeting, discussing if we preferred a home with four bedrooms, where each boy had his own room, or if we wanted a three-bedroom with a bonus room, which would serve as an area for all of them and their friends when they came to visit. Honestly, I knew I couldn't afford four bedrooms and a bonus room. A place to live was a huge question mark in our life. We didn't get an immediate answer to this question mark, but it was in the waiting that I learned to cast my cares on God. Clinging to Him was my only hope. A fresh start for the four of us in a new house was the desire of my heart; however, I had absolutely no clue how it was going to happen.

There are times while walking the journey of divorce you'll feel hopeless. You'll want to give up and throw in the towel. Dreaming feels impossible. How do you keep going on the days when you feel like God isn't close?

We're going to pop in and visit those Israelites once again. The Israelites had safely crossed the Jordan. I really love what they did next.

So Joshua called together the twelve men he had chosen—one from each of the tribes of Israel. He told them, "Go into the middle of the Jordan, in front of the Ark of the LORD your God. Each of you must pick up one stone and carry it out on your shoulder—twelve stones in all, one for each of the twelve tribes of Israel. We will use these stones to build a memorial. In the future your children will ask you, 'What do these stones mean?' Then you can tell them, 'They remind us that the Jordan River stopped flowing when the

Ark of the LORD's Covenant went across.' These stones will stand as a memorial among the people of Israel forever."

Joshua 4:4–7

Then this. This part gets me!

So the men did as Joshua had commanded them. They took twelve stones from the middle of the Jordan River, one for each tribe, just as the LORD had told Joshua. They carried them to the place where they camped for the night and constructed the memorial there.

Joshua also set up another pile of twelve stones in the middle of the Jordan, at the place where the priests who carried the Ark of the Covenant were standing. And they are there to this day.

Joshua 4:8–9

That part gets me because, as a human, I would want to place the stones of remembrance where I arrived—in my case, in the new house of my dreams. After I get through the difficult season and know the solution. I would have placed those stones on the Promised Land–side of the river, the side they had been waiting forty years for. But no! God instructed Joshua to put the stones where they had been, on the miraculous path they had walked through the Jordan. Not just at the end of the journey, when their feet were on dry land, but also along the middle of the journey.

This was a great reminder for me during my house search. God didn't want me to wait until my feet were inside a new home. He wanted me to put down stones before I got there. He wanted me to keep walking the miraculous path He was creating for the boys and for me. He wanted me to know that He takes care of me in ways I can't even begin to imagine. He wanted His best for the four of us.

In March of 2017 I was at a point where I was finally beginning the journey of healing from all that had been lost in my life, beginning to find myself again, and finally feeling like I could move forward, but I had this huge question mark in my life. I needed to move into a new home. The boys and I needed a place for new memories and a fresh start. But where I live, right outside of Nashville, the real estate market is highly competitive, and my budget was comparatively small.

On a Thursday, I woke up empty. So much had been lost. Mediation for my divorce had been the day before, and mediation is physically and emotionally exhausting. That morning was one of those mornings when I just wanted to crawl back in bed and pull the covers over my head. But I didn't; I got up, got all three kids off to school, and hopped in the shower.

And I stood there crying, weeping, and praying. My prayer was super simple: I prayed for twenty-four hundred square feet. That was my entire prayer. It wasn't fancy, didn't follow any catchy prayer acronyms, and didn't include Scripture. I just repeatedly said, "God, I need twenty-four hundred square feet," over and over and over as tears fell. I don't even know where I got the number twenty-four hundred . . . or why twenty-four hundred was my ask. But I pleaded to God for twenty-four hundred square feet that day. Twenty-four hundred square feet was a number I had never said out loud to myself or anyone else before.

Since I couldn't stand in the shower and cry all day, I got ready and headed out to run a few errands, and it was about two hours later when I was walking into a yoga studio that my phone buzzed. On my screen was a text message from a number I didn't know, a phone number that wasn't in my contacts. The text message simply said, "Hi Brandi, this is Polly, we have a mutual friend. I heard you were looking for a house in my neighborhood and I was just on a walk and ran into a neighbor who told me they found out they are being transferred out of state and are selling their house. Are you interested in seeing it? I don't know much about it except"—you guessed it—"it is twenty-four hundred square feet."

In that moment I knew, *God, you hear me. You know what I need, you know.* Whether it was that home or another one, I knew God was listening. He knew the desires of my heart. I wasn't alone.

I walked through that home three or four days later and immediately knew it would be our fresh start. My confidence in God's provision for us was so strong that after that initial visit I immediately ordered address labels that said "The Wilson Family" with the address of that home. Ten days later I had a contract on that 2,400-square-foot house; it never hit our competitive real estate market and came in right at my budget. It's the house where my sons and I have lived since 2017, and it is our house of truth.

Our home is our biggest stone of remembrance. Not a day goes by that I don't pull into my driveway and remember the gift of God's provision for my family. Our home is safe and cozy. Our home is a house of truth. Love lives here. Our home is now full of laughter and beautiful memories. Our home is a reminder that God goes before us.

In the middle of our questions.

In the middle of uncertainty.

He knows what follows the end of our marriage.

He knows the path we walk.

During my divorce I spent many hours facedown on my bedroom floor in prayer, begging and pleading. I begged for God to heal my circumstances and learned that what He really wanted to heal was me. I pleaded for Him to show me what was going to happen, and He taught me to trust Him. I wanted the waiting to end, and He carried me through. I begged Him to restore and redeem my marriage. I desired my life to be tied up in a pretty, restored bow, and He graciously redeemed and restored *me*.

Begin to dream for yourself again. Take some time and reflect on who you are and what you're learning about yourself. Think on things you used to love, as I did with my horses, and pray about incorporating them back into your life. Ask yourself: *What do I envision when I think about my future? What are three bite-size dreams I can make happen in the next three to four months?*

Recently I walked a group of newly divorced women through these exercises on dreaming. The night we met to share our dreams, the countenances of the attendees shifted. Where most weeks had included tears and struggles, this night opened with smiles. There was excitement on the face of each woman as she shared what she wanted for her future. From career to family to relationships, each had recorded a dream she had and steps of how to make the dream a reality.

- One lady loved camping but hadn't camped in years because her ex-husband hated to camp. She had already started a savings account to purchase a camper to begin camping with her kids.
- Another member of the group is a travel agent and is working to get sponsors to provide some time away for women who have gone through the stress of a failed marriage and divorce so they can rest and recuperate via a cruise vacation.
- One mom who loves to travel internationally booked her first trip to take her kids abroad that summer. She had a dream to pass on her love of travel to her children.

Life has a way of balancing out tragedy with abounding beauty. The tragic shapes us and forces us to grow. In the tragic, we develop our resilience and dependence on God. The tragedy helps us expand our capacity for healing, increase our emotional intelligence, and recognize that we are stronger than we ever believed. And the truth is, the beautiful and the tragic are often in a harmonious dance. They are aligned together in a way that reminds us what's really important in life. They remind us of our Christ-given ability to heal—a tedious process that includes smiles and tears, forgiveness and grace, and tender hearts and strong backs. And what is our role? Our role is to trust the process of growth and healing, to trust ourselves, and to trust in His good promises.

Some steps toward healing and dreaming feel huge, like purchasing a new home for a fresh new start. And some steps feel small in comparison, like the simple recognition of the value of writing down a list to get your thoughts in order and begin to dream again. Yet all the steps toward healing, growth, and self-awareness matter. They are all significant, empowering, and worthy of your hard work.

Better Than Okay
Is Just the Beginning

How to Live and Love Your New Life

You've reached the last chapter, and I truly hope you're beginning to feel better than okay. As difficult as your journey has been thus far, you're still standing, still growing, and still moving forward one step and one day at a time. There are gonna be times when you suddenly seem to have taken steps backward, that you've lost all you had gained. On those days, you need to remember healing is not a straight line. Setbacks and stumbling blocks are to be expected. When those circumstances are taunting you, stop and remind yourself: What you have accomplished, *you* have accomplished. What you have gained, *you* have gained. What you have overcome, *you* have overcome. As those circumstances pass, you'll realize you're not starting from the beginning, you're starting from where you left off.

Your past isn't something to leave behind and never revisit. Your past has crafted what you value. Your past has taught you how to dream. Your past has reminded you what you deserve. Your past has strengthened you and given you depth of character.

Some of you are still allowing your past to hold you hostage. Your past is keeping you from experiencing true freedom. A big reason we can't get past our past is us. We can't get out of our own way. When your past resurfaces and tries to drag you down, when your past is shouting you're not good enough, when your past is mocking you and saying that life will never get better, I want you to remember that there is a past version of you that would be so proud of how far you've come.

We often have a hard time recognizing the benefits of our past, because our past contains hurt and disappointment and people who rejected us. Our past has loss, death, betrayal, unfulfilled dreams, broken relationships, and unmet expectations. There's a long list of things in our past that hold us back.

My past is full of things that could hold me back. My marriage wasn't supposed to have trust repeatedly shattered; I never thought I'd be divorced after nearly twenty years of marriage and have to step away from a church I loved and had led for fourteen years. And then add the embarrassment and gossip of people watching my life fall apart publicly. I never expected to be dating at forty-eight. There are many times I've stopped and said aloud to myself, "What happened to my life? What the heck happened?"

And that's when I have to anchor myself in God's story, because that is where my story makes sense. Let's take a look at one of my favorite passages in Isaiah 61. As you are reading this first part, I want you to pay attention if any of this language (anyone else's life feel like a ruin?) feels like your life or maybe describes your past.

They will rebuild the ancient ruins,
    repairing cities destroyed long ago.
They will revive them,
    though they have been deserted for many
        generations. . . .
Instead of shame and dishonor,
    you will enjoy a double share of honor.
    You will possess a double portion of prosperity in your
        land,
    and everlasting joy will be yours.
"For I, the LORD, love justice.
    I hate robbery and wrongdoing.
I will faithfully reward my people for their suffering
    and make an everlasting covenant with them.
Their descendants will be recognized
    and honored among the nations.
Everyone will realize that they are a people
    the LORD has blessed."

Isaiah 61:4, 7–9

We're going to be working our way through this passage, because what Isaiah 61 is telling us is that when we move forward from our past into the freedom God has promised, He has some incredible and unthinkable results in store for us. Things beyond what we can imagine.

How do we get there? How do we receive the double share of honor, the double portion of prosperity, the everlasting joy? How do we become the people the Lord has blessed? How do we get past our past?

Because we get stuck sometimes. We feel more shame and dishonor than honor. We operate more in doubt than prosperity, and there are times when grief outweighs joy.

Embrace honor

Instead of shame and dishonor,
you will enjoy a double share of honor.

Isaiah 61:7

God doesn't just want us to experience honor, He promises a double share! He wants us to embrace the honor He's bestowed on us.

A moment of blunt honesty. Nothing pushes me to a point where I dishonor myself more than when someone takes my phone charger. Y'all, it's a struggle. I'm sure you've found yourself in a similar situation. You're busy working and you notice your phone is in the red! That's where the anxiety begins. You hustle over to the designated plug in the kitchen, reach for the cord . . . and the designated charger is gone. Gone like the wind.

At my house, I label that sucker with a label from my label maker (judge me if you want, yes, I own and use a label maker) that says MOM (yes, in all caps like I'm yelling, 'cause I am). When I discover my charger is gone, I threaten lives and turn into a crazy woman. All because a white, one-inch cube and eighteen-inch cord have disappeared from my life! Their grubby boy hands have snatched MOM's charger.

Sometimes I go on the wild goose chase to find my well-labeled charger. I dig through their rooms, look at the plugs behind the couch in the bonus room. And sometimes I act really immature and stand by my designated plug in the kitchen and yell, "WHO HAS MY CHARGER?" repeatedly. It's embarrassing to admit the fits I've thrown over a phone charger. I'm believing I'm not alone.

There are other more serious ways we dishonor and shame ourselves.

We compare ourselves to someone else.

We work harder at our digital lives than we do at our real lives.

We focus on what is going wrong more than what is going right.

We deny we've experienced heartbreak and trudge ahead.

Then there is shame and dishonor that has been put on us by another individual. Words that have been spoken over us that we believe. Words that crush our heart and remove our focus from Jesus. Actions that cause us to believe we're not worthy of love.

A double share of honor is yours for the taking. Embracing the honor He has promised us may not be something you're used to. But now is the time to walk into your new life. Time to lean into where you see God at work around you and cooperate with the new He has for you. Now is the time to shake off the shame that has shackled you for far too long. You aren't going back, you're moving forward. The past is a powerful teacher, and you're choosing to live life bold and brave.

Expect God's prosperity

> You will possess a double portion of prosperity in your
> land . . .
>
> Isaiah 61:7

When my boys were younger, we went on a mission trip in the Dominican Republic. It was an incredible experience, and we spent the last couple of days at an all-inclusive resort. It was their first all-inclusive experience, and it was about halfway through the first day when they discovered the swim-up bar. The swim-up bar at an all-inclusive resort was the definition of prosperity for them. I can't tell you how many Sprites they kicked back that day, but I can tell you I snapped approximately one hundred thirty-seven photos of them doggie paddling across the pool, holding their soda in the air out of the water, grinning from ear to ear!

"You will possess a double portion of SODA prosperity in your land" is how my boys believed Isaiah 61:7 read.

Prosperity is not about attaining wealth or living a life of luxury, but about thriving as the person God created you to be. We should expect prosperity in our lives. God wants us to thrive. He wants me to thrive. He wants you to thrive. True prosperity is about living a life fully engaged with His principles and teachings.

Life is hard. I get tired. There are a lot of details to manage in life.

People complain about what I cook for dinner (*people* being my children).

Bills need to be paid.

Homework needs to be checked.

Curriculum needs to be written.

Bathrooms need to be cleaned.

Work needs to be completed.

Dreams need to be chased.

I'm pulled in a million directions. I'm guessing your life looks similar, and you get tired too. Sometimes, in the midst of life and taking care of all the details, I begin to doubt.

I move from a posture of being upright and full of honor, expecting prosperity, to being slumped over. And I allow the details, decisions, and drama to weigh me down.

I move from this posture of being upright and full of honor to being hunched over. But don't forget friend, we no longer live life bent.

I'm living life full of doubt, expecting failure instead of prosperity. But God is the lifter of our heads, and He gives us the honor of being His children. He has called me. He has called you.

He didn't restore you just to refuse you.

He didn't do a miracle just to mess with you.

He didn't heal you just to leave you out to dry.

He didn't open a door just to disappear.

He didn't meet your needs just to ignore them now.

He didn't accept you just to reject you.

He didn't offer you grace just to refuse you help.

He didn't find you just to forget you.

He didn't make you just to break you.

He didn't renew you just to refuse you.

How do these truths change our countenance when we're discouraged and doubting? My initial instinct is to look to myself to be self-sufficient. Y'all, that's exhausting. It kicks up my anxiety, and instead of embracing faith for my future, I quickly trade it away for fear.

Recently I was working with a personal coach processing some business decisions and personal struggles, and he asked me a simple question: "Who takes care of you?"

Immediately my eyes filled with tears.

My response to him was, "I know the 'correct' answer is God, but it feels like I'm the only one who takes care of me."

I don't know about you, but sometimes life feels very singular. Very "if I don't take care of myself, no one will." It's a personal struggle, but I also think it's a struggle of humanity.

Expecting prosperity in life means resting in His arms:

Allowing Him to take care of you, comfort your tender heart, and refresh your tired soul

Reminding yourself that God takes care of you

Remembering you're not alone in this journey of life

Writing it in your journal

Putting it on a Post-it on your bathroom mirror

Praying it repeatedly as you drive down the road

For me, it's writing it over and over in my journal, like sentences on a chalkboard, so it sticks. The repetition helps make that truth the first thing that takes over my thinking when I begin to wonder how my life will play out. It's in these moments of my doubt, when I'm discouraged, when I'm battling a setback, that I look up and see again what He's done, what He's given, how He's provided for me and my boys.

The same is true for you.

Take your gaze and raise your head to focus on Him. Set your eyes on Him, and ready your ears to listen. Be expectant for His prosperity in your life. Remember that He's taken care of you before, and He'll take care of you again.

Embody joy

> . . . and everlasting joy will be yours.
>
> Isaiah 61:7

When I was a tween, I'm pretty sure I defined joy by Barbara Mandrell concerts, *Saved by the Bell*, Little Debbie Swiss Rolls, and Guess jeans. But as I grew up and started living the adult life, joy was a lot harder to find.

Joy disappeared while walking through divorce. My life fell apart, and divorce devastated the family I dreamed of. My kids and I worked hard together to redefine our family unit. There were tears, fights, sleepless nights, difficult conversations, and more questions than answers. And slowly joy began to seep back into our lives. There started to be more smiles than tears, more laughter than silence, and more love than disappointment.

Did I want divorce to be part of my story? No.

Did I want divorce to be part of my kids' life? Absolutely not!

Would I change where we are today? Not on your life.

We're incredibly close and always available for one another. We're messy and beautiful together. We're family, and nothing's missing. This is my everlasting joy and double portion. The relationship I have with my boys is my double portion. My family is my double portion.

It isn't necessarily what I thought my double portion would look like. I honestly thought my double portion would mean I might be remarried by now. I thought my double portion would mean my kids got to live in a home where they could see a healthy marriage, one where they could experience a husband respect and love his wife.

But because we're human, we often look more at what we lack than what we have. When we look at what we lack, we create in our minds what our double portion will look like, thinking, *This is what I lack; therefore, if God were to double my portion, He'd double my lack.*

Double portion rarely looks like what we thought. A double portion isn't what we lost times two—it's so much more. It isn't two spoonfuls of mashed potatoes, look how lucky I am. It isn't just a second dessert. Yay me! (I'll admit, I'm hoping my double portion is about 6'2" and handsome.)

My double portion is a loving and open relationship with my boys. Having conversations that are truthful. Seeing my boys grow in their relationship with Christ and learn to lean in to Him.

My double portion is living the truth that a role or a title might be taken away, but no one can take away God's call on my life.

My double portion is continuing to be able to do ministry.

My double portion is starting a coaching business where my suffering can be a survival guide for others.

My double portion is helping other women know they're going to make it. Reminding them they might be damaged but not destroyed. Helping them make sense of their story.

My double portion is leaning in to my giftings and thriving as who God created me to be.

My double portion is a life of contentment and everlasting joy.

I couldn't have pictured what that looked like on the other side of grief. I couldn't have imagined how beautiful my life would be post-divorce. I couldn't have foreseen the amount of freedom healing would bring to my life.

My double portion isn't what I thought—it's better!

The irony is, our double portion feels better *because* of what we've lost.

Because of our pain and our heartache.

Because of our grief.

That's what's so beautiful about the language of the text in Isaiah 61—the rebuilding is active, it takes work, there is sweat. Physical labor has to go into rebuilding it. God was restoring *and* people had to get up and go to work. We all heal and rebuild differently. We have different circumstances, different variables, different pasts, and different pains. But God's promises remain the same. He is a God who wants to partner with you as you rebuild your life.

The past version of you would be so proud of how far you've come. That past version of you had a powerful role in you becoming the person you are today. The adversity you've conquered. The damage you've fought to heal. The hard times you've walked through and kept going. The suffering you've experienced. And still you trust Him, and still you grow. Because God takes care of you, and God takes care of me.

Let me remind you what He promises in Isaiah:

> For I, the LORD, love justice.
>   I hate robbery and wrongdoing.
> I will faithfully reward my people for their suffering
>   and make an everlasting covenant with them.
> Their descendants will be recognized
>   and honored among the nations.
> Everyone will realize that they are a people
>   the LORD has blessed.
>   Isaiah 61:8–9

I'm gonna rephrase Isaiah 61, verse 9 a bit: *All who see YOU will acknowledge that YOU are a person the Lord has blessed.* Take a second and repeat that to yourself. Feel it in your soul. Say it out loud. You are a person the Lord has blessed.

———————————

Due to the wonders of technology, one of my sons recently heard me speak at our Leading and Loving It conference. As part of my message that day, I shared my story as well as how God had showed up and partnered with me in big and small ways. I wanted the audience to be aware that hope and healing were possible in their lives too. The message wrapped up with me stating what I shared above. I never wanted divorce to be part of my story. I never wanted divorce to be part of my kids' story. However, standing on the other side of divorce, I can honestly say I wouldn't change my life for anything.

After that message, I popped back to the green room and grabbed my phone to see I had a few text messages from one person—my son, who had watched from over seventeen hundred miles away. He offered some encouragement about my jokes and the audience's response. But the text that stood out the most was the one that said, "I agree, I wouldn't change our lives for anything."

That text from my son gave me a new kind of peace. It helped me remember how God had been with me every step of the way, and how even though it had been the hardest work of my life, I had come this far. And my son was bearing witness to it.

If I could, I'd send you a text message right now. But I'll do the next best thing. I will write you a permission slip right here, inside this book, as you take these next life-changing steps on your own journey forward. Our circumstances are different, but the core truths are the same: Isaiah 61 is a promise for both of us.

Friend, remember, the you from the past would be so proud of how far you've come. You never expected to be here, walking this path of a failed marriage, but you have the opportunity to put the pieces of your life back together the way you want them. You're in control. You're going to find yourself laughing more. You're going to feel lighter. You'll realize you don't remember the last time you cried. You'll stop feeling fragile and begin to recognize your resilience. You'll be proud of who you are and how you're growing. As you've turned the pages of this book, you've started to recognize yourself again, you've seen glimpses of what your future could be, and anticipation and excitement are stirring in your soul. You're brave enough to face the grief and courageous enough to shed the shame.

And one day, maybe much to your surprise, you may pass a handsome man and immediately check to see if he's wearing a wedding ring; that's a pretty good sign you're ready to begin dating. Go for it. Before you open the door of the restaurant to meet him, pause and give yourself a little pep talk. He is so lucky to get to spend the next sixty minutes with you!

Or maybe one day you'll wake up and realize the life you're living is better than what you've dreamed, regardless of your relationship status.

Your life isn't over. You're not ruined. Begin dreaming about your next best steps, how you can walk freely into all that is in store for the days ahead. You will survive your divorce and come out stronger!

Better than okay is just the beginning. You're just getting started, and I can't wait to hear how you choose to live and love your new life.

Books That Guided My Healing Process

The Inner Voice of Love: A Journey Through Anguish to Freedom by Henri J. M. Nouwen

The Body Keeps the Score: Brain, Mind, and Body in the Healing of Trauma by Bessel van der Kolk

Forgiving What You Can't Forget: Discover How to Move On, Make Peace with Painful Memories, and Create a Life That's Beautiful by Lysa TerKeurst

Why Does He Do That? Inside the Minds of Angry and Controlling Men by Lundy Bancroft

Try Softer: A Fresh Approach to Move Us out of Anxiety, Stress, and Survival Mode—and into a Life of Connection and Joy by Aundi Kolber

Boundaries for Your Soul: How to Turn Your Overwhelming Thoughts and Feelings into Your Greatest Allies by Alison Cook and Kimberly Miller

The Forgotten Body: A Way of Knowing and Understanding Self by Elissa Cobb

Living Unbroken: Reclaiming Your Life and Your Heart after Divorce by Tracie Miles

Acknowledgments

Pulling together a list of people who helped this book come to reality feels a lot like making a list of people who loved me back to life. A written thank-you never feels like quite enough.

Jennifer Dukes Lee, you went over and above as an editor. The gentleness with which you handled my story and the value you gave it empowered me to give hope to others. Huge thanks to you and Deirdre Close for trekking down to spend a day with me in Franklin to get this project off the ground. The entire team at Bethany House went over and above to package this story in a way that points back to Him. I'm grateful that they are now considered friends. Thank you Elisa Haugen, Rebecca Schriner, Mycah McKeown, Bria Conway, Brian Brunsting, and Dan Pitts.

Esther Fedorkevich, I'm grateful for your "out of the blue" call a few years ago when you asked if I was healing and ready to share my story. Thank you and everyone at The Fedd Agency for being part of my team.

Kyle Negrete, thank you for valuing the voice of women and helping this project find a home with Bethany House.

Koula Callahan, you showed up for my boys and me in ways I never expected. It all started with chips, queso, an acai bowl, and a bottle of wine. Look how far we've come. Thank you for showing up then and for continuing to show up now.

Stephen, Jackie, Isaiah, Ashlyn, Hope, and Grace Brewster, you guys are lifers. You've taken me in on holidays, shown up at games, and dedicated an entire evening of your week to "Brandi and the Brewsters." I love each of you.

Taylor Ann Dietrich, I never expected my kids' first-grade teacher to become one of my dearest friends. I'm grateful our Sunday chats deepened our friendship and that there were always loving eyes on my kids while they were at school with you.

Kerlin, your presence has been the sweetest addition to our family. You're a gift. Thank you for invading our nest.

Rodes and Page, you guys were the best stand-in big brother and big sister a girl could have. You protected, guided, and loved me in ways that can't be counted. Thank you.

The Six Pack, how would I have survived Friday Night Lights without you ladies? The reality that our friendship has continued long after the high school football careers of our sons ended is a true gift in my life.

Cross Point Church, your impact on my life for fourteen years will never be forgotten. I'm still cheering you on and have been so proud of the way you continue to make an impact in Middle Tennessee.

John and Kristin Ragsdale and The Hills, thank you for being a safe place for the four of us to land. John, I'll never forget the prayer you prayed over Gage at his baptism and the prayer you prayed over all four of us the day you guys opened your new building. Those are memory-making moments that were God ordained and won't be forgotten.

Local Church, you've made this megachurch gal love the microchurch world. Your intentional community gave me a place to feel at home in church again.

Mom, Dad, and Jeremy, your love gave me the foundation I needed to survive and continue to grow. Words will never be enough. I know your heart was broken alongside mine and many prayers were lifted on our behalf. Thank you for being the original Us Four.

My outlaws (formerly known as in-laws), thank you for loving me like family for twenty years and not allowing divorce to destroy that love. Sue, the relationship we have is something I will always cherish.

Leading and Loving It community, you guys sent texts, prayers, and messages to me on the days I didn't want to keep going. Thank you for being such a safe place for me to use my voice the first time and continuing to cheer me on.

The Core Four, you've picked up the balls I've dropped as I've been writing. There isn't a better team around, and I love working with each of you. Just wish we could have coffee more often face-to-face. Thank you for being real women of grit and grace.

Diane Marshall, thank you for being a therapist turned friend. You walked me through the darkest times of my life with gentleness, honesty, and grace. You beautifully guided me toward healing and empowered me at the same time.

Lori Reid and Lindsey, I never expected to become friends with my divorce attorney. You two are golden.

Lori and Jud, David and Lisa, you four are the reason I'm not "damaged" in my relationship with the church. God was sovereign and gracious to give me two incredible pastor families to care for me in such loving ways. Jud and David, thank you for being men, leaders, husbands, fathers, and pastors of integrity. Lisa, your wisdom mixed with a wicked sense of humor is legendary.

Lori, honestly, where do I begin? You weren't only a best friend, you pastored me through the deepest lows. If "support person" was in the dictionary, there would be a photo of you. Your daily phone calls to hear my voice and your patience in my grief taught me what true friendship is. You guarded me, guided me, were a guru and part of my gang all at the same time. Thank you for sitting in so many seats at my table.

Jett, Gage, and Brewer, the bond we share is one of my greatest joys. Together we walked a devastating story. This book exists because of you. I'm not telling my story; I'm recording our story and how we found hope and healing together. I'm sure our family will grow in the future, but I'll always cherish being Us 4.

Notes

Introduction

1. Jen Todd and Holly Meyer, "Cross Point Church Pastor Pete Wilson Resigns After 14 Years," *The Tennessean*, September 11, 2016, https://www.tennessean.com/story/news/religion/2016/09/11/cross-point-church-pastor-pete-wilson-resigns-after-14-years/90233854/.

Chapter 1: To Be Continued . . .

1. Henri J. M. Nouwen, *The Inner Voice of Love: A Journey Through Anguish to Freedom* (United Kingdom: Crown Publishing Group, 2010), 34–35.

Chapter 3: I Cussed a Lot

1. Allison Fallon, *The Power of Writing It Down: A Simple Habit to Unlock Your Brain and Reimagine Your Life* (Grand Rapids: Zondervan, 2020), 4–5.

Chapter 5: Whose Voice Do You Hear?

1. David A. Sbarra, Hillary L. Smith, and Matthias R. Mehl, "When Leaving Your Ex, Love Yourself: Observational Ratings of Self-Compassion Predict the Course of Emotional Recovery Following Marital Separation," *Psychological Science* 23, no. 3 (March 2012): 261-9, https://journals.sagepub.com/doi/10.1177/0956797611429466

Chapter 6: I've Never Missed My Ex

1. "Scientists Show What Loneliness Looks Like in the Brain," *Genetic Engineering and Biotechnology News*, December 16, 2020, https://www.genengnews.com/news/scientists-show-what-loneliness-looks-like-in-the-brain/.

Chapter 7: Humbly Grateful or Grumbly Hateful

1. Luna Greenstein, "When Looking for Happiness, Find Gratitude," National Alliance on Mental Illness, September 23, 2016, https://www.nami.org/Blogs/NAMI-Blog/September-2016/When-Looking-for-Happiness-Find-Gratitude.

2. Maanvi Singh, "If You Feel Thankful, Write It Down. It's Good For Your Health," NPR News, December 24, 2018, https://www.npr.org/sections/health-shots/2018/12/24/678232331/if-you-feel-thankful-write-it-down-its-good-for-your-health.

3. Luna Greenstein, "When Looking for Happiness, Find Gratitude."

4. Robi Sonderegger, "Five Character Traits to Grow through Trauma," (lecture, Fearless Mom Conference, Austin, TX, February 26, 2022).

Chapter 8: Out of his Shadow

1. Krista Smith, "Exclusive: Jennifer Garner's Frank Talk About Kids, Men, and Ben Affleck," *Vanity Fair*, February 26, 2016, https://www.vanityfair.com/hollywood/2016/02/jennifer-garner-talks-kids-career-ben-affleck.

Chapter 9: My "Ex-Husband Knots"

1. Koula Callahan, "Impact of Mindful Movement on the Brain," (lecture, Self-Care Workshop, Nashville, TN, February 8–9, 2019).

2. Bessel van der Kolk, *The Body Keeps the Score: Brain, Mind, and Body in the Healing of Trauma* (New York: Penguin, 2014), 97.

3. Van der Kolk, *The Body Keeps the Score*, 132.

Chapter 10: "I Googled Dad"

1. Bill Lokey, "Family Map Exercise," (lecture, Onsite; Living Centered Program, Cumberland Furnace, TN, January 9, 2018).

2. Nicole Smith, "What to Say (and Not to Say) to Your Children in a Divorce," *SurviveDivorce.com*, https://www.survivedivorce.com/what-to-tell-children-divorce.

Chapter 11: Us Four, No More

1. Kelly McGonigal, *The Upside of Stress: Why Stress is Good for You, and How to Get Good at It* (New York: Penguin, 2016), 70.

Chapter 12: I Have a Six Pack and I Don't Mean My Abs

1. Lissa Rankin, MD, "The Healing Power of Telling Your Story," *Psychology Today*, November 27, 2012, https://www.psychologytoday.com/us/blog/owning-pink/201211/the-healing-power-telling-your-story.

Chapter 14: Stop Trying to Resuscitate What's Dead

1. *This Is Us*, season 2, episode 11, "The Fifth Wheel," written by Dan Fogelman, Vera Herbert, and Kay Oyegun, directed by Chris Koch, aired January 9, 2018, on NBC.

Chapter 15: Brandi Got Her Groove Back

1. *Ted Lasso*, season 2, episode 1, "Goodbye Earl," written by Jason Sudeikis, Bill Lawrence, and Brendan Hunt, directed by Declan Lowney, aired on July 23, 2021, on AppleTV.

Brandi Wilson is an author, certified coach, and speaker who lives in Nashville, Tennessee. She has been part of two church plants, the most recent being Cross Point Church in Nashville, where she served for fourteen years. For more than a decade Brandi has been involved in leadership at Leading and Loving It, a nonprofit created to empower women to love life and ministry. Brandi is passionate about walking alongside single moms as they navigate parenting and life. When Brandi isn't following one of her three teenage sons to a practice or sporting event, she enjoys yoga, hiking, gardening, and time spent with friends. She loves all things cozy and comfortable and works hard to craft a simple life she loves living. Learn more at lovebrandiwilson.com.